RETRO ROADMAP®

Cool Vintage Places & Retro Fun with Mod Betty!
www.RetroRoadmap.com

Pennsylvania: Philadephia Suburbs

Including *Bucks, Chester, Delaware and Montgomery Counties*

Sabrina —
Happy Retro Roadmapping!
MOD BETTY

COVER DESIGN: KATHY KIKKERT
LAYOUT & TEXT DESIGN: BETH LENNON & LISA KATARYNICK
AUTHOR PHOTO (AND 1955 CHEVROLET BEL AIR) BY KEN LEBLANC
ALL CONTENT AND PHOTOGRAPHY: BETH LENNON, UNLESS OTHERWISE INDICATED

Published by Retro Roadmap Roadbooks

A Mod Betty® Production

Dedicated to Retro Roadhusband Cliff Hillis, the best sidekick a girl could ever ask for, Rigby the Retro Roaddog for ensuring I don't sit at my desk for too long, and my family and friends for accompanying me on visits to diners, bowling alleys and roadside attractions whenever we get together.

Heartfelt thanks to Retro Roadmappers everywhere - who help keep the cool vintage places we love so much alive, not only online but in real life!

A Few Technical Details:

Scan The Stamp:

Those little stamp shaped boxes on each place page contain a QR ("Quick Response") code, linking directly to the RetroRoadmap.com writeup for that location. If you have/get a QR code scanner on your mobile phone all you need to do is "scan the stamp" and the spot will appear on your phone. Then simply click the orange button that says "Get Google Map Directions to This Spot" and voila! you can easily navigate to that location via Google Maps without having to type the address in manually.

A Friendly Reminder:

The information (including website addresses and phone numbers) in this book was up-to-date when we sent it to the printer, but with vintage places, things can change at any time. To save yourself frustration (been there!) make sure to call before you head to any of these locations - to ensure they will be open when you want to visit.

If you learn that one of these locations has sadly closed for good (or done away with its "authentic vintage charm") please drop me a note at modbetty@retroroadmap.com so I can update RetroRoadmap.com. Thanks for being a Retro Roadmapper!

The List
Check Off Your Progress!

Bucks County

To Do

- ❏ Bucks County Playhouse
- ❏ County Theater
- ❏ Newtown Theatre
- ❏ Perkasie Carousel
- ❏ Sellersville Theater

To Eat

- ❏ Warner's Candies
- ❏ Washington House Restaurant

To Shop

- ❏ Newtown Hardware House
- ❏ Sine's 5 & 10 Store

To Stay

- ❏ Washington House Hotel

Chester County

To Do

- ❏ Colonial Theatre

To Eat

- ❏ DeStarr's Restaurant
- ❏ DK Diner
- ❏ Fisherman Restaurant
- ❏ Frazer Diner
- ❏ G Lodge Restaurant
- ❏ Miss Oxford Diner

To Shop

- ❏ Baldwin's Book Barn
- ❏ Lulu Boutique & Gifterie
- ❏ Malena's Vintage Boutique

Delaware County

To Do

- ❏ Anthony Wayne Theater
- ❏ Media Theatre
- ❏ Philadelphia Skating Club
- ❏ Tower Theater

To Eat

- ❏ Chung Sing Restaurant
- ❏ Hungry A
- ❏ Jimmy John's
- ❏ Original Thunderbird
- ❏ R. Weinrich German Bakery

To Shop

- ❏ Booths Corner Market
- ❏ Deals Variety Store

Montgomery County

To Do

- ❏ Ambler Theater
- ❏ Beth Sholom Synagogue
- ❏ Bryn Mawr Film Institute
- ❏ Grand Theater
- ❏ Hiway Theater
- ❏ Keswick Theatre
- ❏ Waltz Golf Farm

To Eat

- ❏ Bergin's Chocolates
- ❏ Blue Comet Bar & Grill
- ❏ Costa Deli
- ❏ Daddypops Diner
- ❏ Danish Bakers
- ❏ Edwards Freeman Nuts
- ❏ Hill Top Drive-In Restaurant
- ❏ Lou's Sandwiches
- ❏ Speck's Drive In Restaurant
- ❏ Stutz Candy

To Shop

- ❏ Abington Pharmacy & Gift
- ❏ Burdick's News Agency
- ❏ Ott's Exotic Plants
- ❏ Weitzenkorn's Men's Store

Beth Lennon aka Mod Betty®

About the Author

Beth Lennon (aka Mod Betty®) is the creative mind behind RetroRoadmap.com / the online source for "Cool Vintage Places & Retro Fun!"

A "Jane of All Trades" she has written for the *National Trust for Historic Preservation*, crowd-sourced funds and starred in the online Retro Roadmap® video series, hostessed meetups and vintage weekends and delivered presentations both serious and silly, across multiple states. Featured in the *Boston Globe*, *Huffington Post* and WHYY-TV, when not on the road 'sploring, she's researching her next roadtrip while seated at the table in her vintage 1964 camper. Have a retro travel tip? Drop her a line at modbetty@retroroadmap.com.

Acknowledgements

This Philadelphia Suburbs Retro Roadmap® Roadbook would not be as complete nor as interesting without the research and help of other like-minded Retro Roadmappers who are doing their part in keeping these cool old places alive.

Special thanks go out to the authors of Diners of Pennsylvania (Brian Butko, Kevin Patrick, Kyle Weaver) who created one of the most oft-referred to resources for this book, and the ever thorough photo documentation of Debra Jane Selzer / RoadsideArchitecture.com.
As Mod Betty says, "Every Little Bit Helps!"

Introduction

Growing up in a house filled with antiques and maps, it seems that I was destined to have a fondness for history and geography. However it wasn't until I was in my teens that I really began to discover what places and things really excited me: Give me a neon sign and a soda fountain over a trip to a colonial-era fancy home any time! Old theaters, clam shacks, 5 &10s - that kind of history is what really got me going, and I started snapping photos of these places almost as soon as I saved up enough gift money to get my very first 35mm film camera.

Fast forward to today, and even though many things have changed about me and the world, what hasn't changed is my love for this type of uniquely American roadside/downtown places. Sadly there are fewer of them than in years past, and they're closing at a rapid rate, with original owners retiring/passing on, and the next generation not interested in the outdated business.

Instead of this causing me defeated resignation about the inevitable "blandification" of the USA (and the world) I'm using this as an energy to get the word out even more quickly about the businesses that still DO exist!

With the flexibility of self-publishing you don't have to wait until I visit an entire state (and run the risk of a place closing before the book is published) before hitting the road, Roadbook in hand. I'm excited to be creating manageable sized resources for you to throw in your car and start having your own adventures as soon as possible!

This ensures that you have the information you need to get on the road sooner, and enjoy these "cool vintage places" while they're still around. Jot down your memories, discover your own finds and faves, and see where other folks have visited, by following the hashtags. The more of us that are out there appreciating these places, the better it is for everyone.

Thanks for being a Retro Roadmapper!
xo- Mod Betty

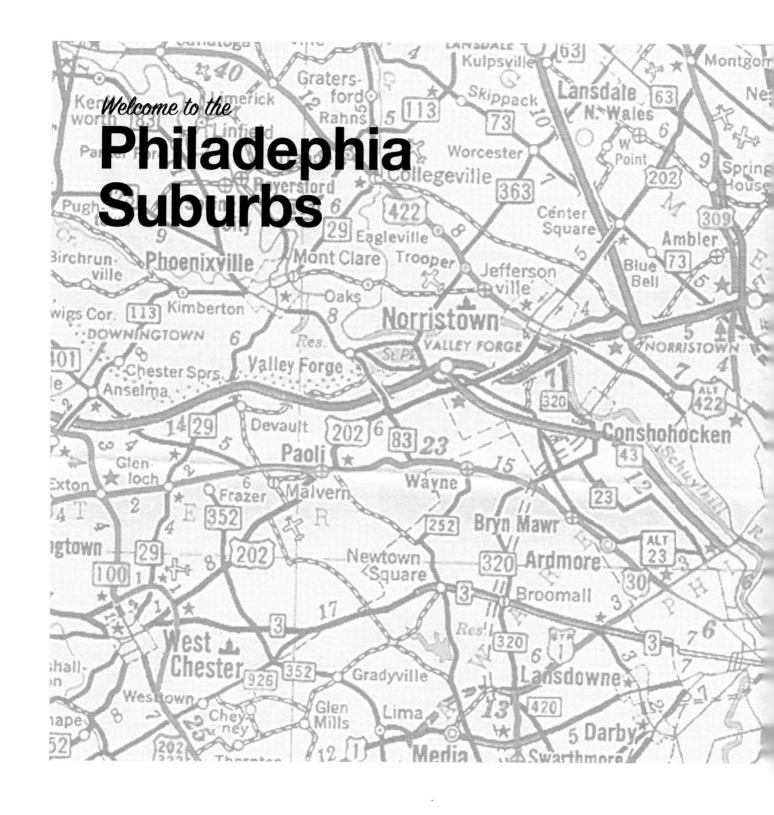

Welcome to the
Philadephia Suburbs

Table of Contents

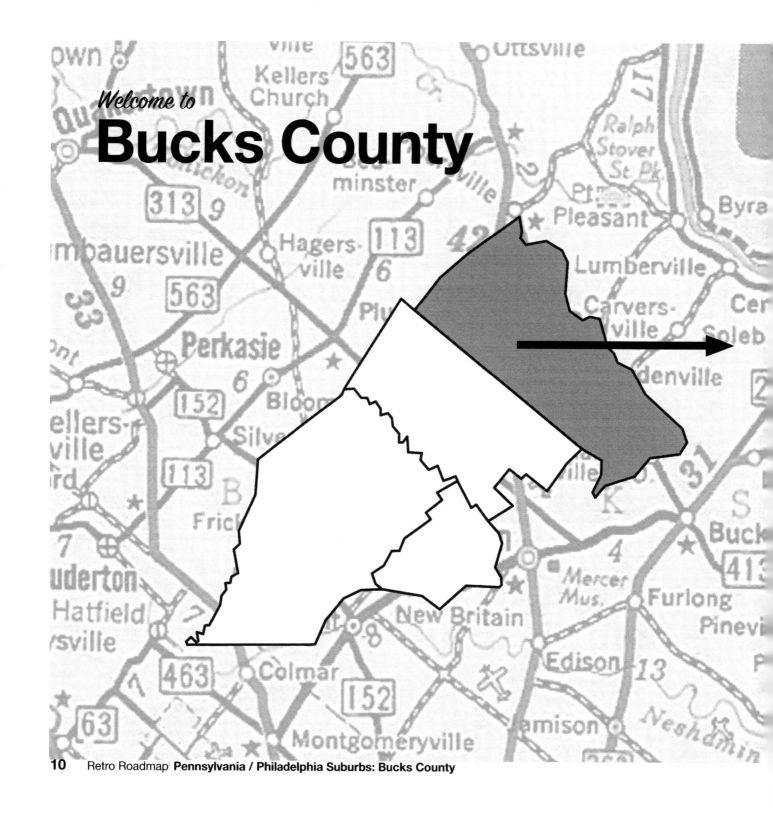

Welcome to
Bucks County

Bucks County

1. Bucks County Playhouse - *New Hope*

2. County Theater - *Doylestown*

3. Newtown Hardware House - *Newtown*

4. Newtown Theatre - *Newtown*

5. Perkasie Carousel - *Perkasie*

6. Sellersville Theater - *Sellersville*

7. Sine's 5 & 10 - *Quakertown*

8. Warner's Candies - *Bensalem*

9. Washington House Restaurant / Hotel - *Sellersville*

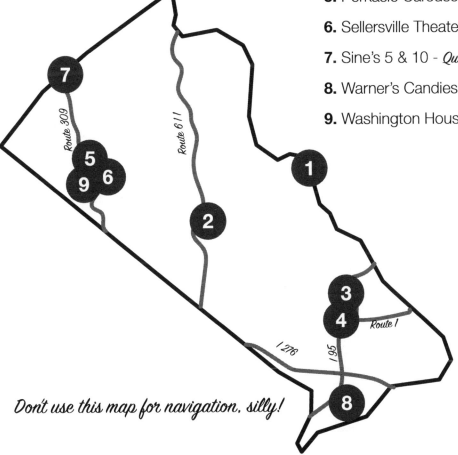

Don't use this map for navigation, silly!

Bucks County Playhouse *New Hope, PA*

Looking like a cheery barn on the banks of the Delaware river in New Hope, the Bucks County Playhouse is a reminder of that famous movie trope, "hey kids, let's put on a show!" as they have been putting on live theater shows here since 1939.

The structure was built in 1790 as a grist mill, harnessing the water power of the adjacent river and picturesque waterfall out front, but in the 1930s it was threatened with demolition. Luckily, during the nineteen-teens and twenties New Hope had become a magnet for artistic and literary types, who were charmed by the bucolic location only 90 minutes from New York City. A group led by Broadway playwright Moss Hart (think The Man Who Came To Dinner, A Star is Born) rallied to help save the building and reimagine it into a theater.

Known as America's Most Famous Summer Theater, it became the launching pad of many a Broadway play and actor's career, including Robert Redford and Grace Kelly. A veritable who's who of stars have trod the stage, including Dick Van Dyke, Bela Lugosi, Angela Lansbury, to name a few.

While the beloved landmark brought world class theater to Bucks County for decades, the years began to take their toll on the building, which, lucky for us, was saved by a local couple and renovated, reopening in 2012. Now open year 'round, there is seating for over 400, exciting new shows, and expanded eating and drinking options for pre-or post-show fun.

Bucks County Playhouse ①

70 S Main St
New Hope, PA 18938
(215) 862-2121

www.bcptheater.org

BUCKS COUNTY

Date: / /

My Visit: _____

_____

_____

_____

_____

_____

_____

_____

_____

_____

_____

_____

_____

_____

Don't forget to check it off The List!

Mod Betty® Says:

❋ *If you're lucky to spy the fire curtain, note - it was painted by Julia Child's brother-in-law, Charles!*

❋ *New Hope is a fun and funky historic town - plan plenty of time to explore Main Street and beyond!*

❋ *Just think of all the famous stars who have entered this historic location - now you're one of `em!*

Scan the Stamp!
for map, website and additional info!

PhillyBurbs

Tag your photos from your visit
#RetroRoadmapPHILLYBURBS

County Theater
Doylestown, PA

Nothing strikes a thrill in the heart of Mod Betty more than the sight of a colorful Art Deco facade, boldly staking a claim in a town's historic look. That is why she's always excited to see the Doylestown PA streetscape enlivened by the sleek blue and yellow exterior of the County Theater, reminding folks that our history encompasses many aesthetic and design modes.

Upon opening in 1939 the theater was not the vibrant spectacle that greets you today, but instead had a more sedate white stucco exterior. The colored enamel panels were added in the 1950s in an effort to appeal to contemporary audiences who were being lured away from downtown theaters towards shopping center cinemas.

As with many downtown theaters, the County had her dark times starting in the 1970s, even going so far as to "twin" the auditorium to expand viewing options in the 1980s.

Lucky for Doylestown and us all, the theater reinvented itself as a non-profit in the early 1990s and the community championed the rebirth of its glamorous downtown gathering space. On the outside the tower sign and marquee were replicated to exact specifications, while inside new seats and screens, as well as digital projection, increases patron comfort.

Much like Mod Betty's home theater the Colonial of Phoenixville, the County has purchased an adjacent business as a way to expand to have more options for the theater. This will ensure the County can continue to offer first-run, art and independent films for years to come.

JANUARY 2019
Open new County Theater Addition.

County Theater ②

20 E State St
Doylestown, PA 18901
(215) 345-6789
www.countytheater.org

Date: / /

My Visit: _____

BUCKS COUNTY

Don't forget to check it off The List!

Mod Betty® Says:

❋ *The tower sign spelling out County is 18 feet tall!*

❋ *Other local theaters related to the County are the Ambler, Hiway and Garden in Princeton NJ*

❋ *That's TheatER not TheatRE :-)*

Scan the Stamp!
for map, website and additional info!

PhillyBurbs

Tag your photos from your visit
#RetroRoadmapPHILLYBURBS

Newtown Hardware House *Newtown, PA*

What is it about the creak of a wooden floor as soon as I set foot into a shop, that sends me back in time? Does this happen to you, too? If so, step foot into Newtown Hardware House in Newtown PA. Not only will you do a bit of time travel, but also come home with all sorts of modern things to keep your contemporary life well repaired.

Located on State Street in the charming little downtown area of Newtown (so charming that the entire business district is on the National Register of Historic Places) this antique hardware store has been in continuous operation at the same location for almost 150 years (opened in 1869 for those who don't want to math.)

The shop is a wonderful mix of antique wooden bins and fixtures filled with nails, screws and the like, but also a heavy helping of gift and toy items with a nostalgic appeal. Cookies are sold to support the local pancreatic cancer fund, keys are made, lamps re-wired too.

Just because it is that old doesn't guarantee its future, but luckily owners Bill and Meg Newell stepped in just a couple of years ago to buy the business, moments before it was slated to close for good. They, as well as many area residents, realized the importance of keeping this place open, for locals to get what they need, and for the younger generation to know what it was like to shop before the big stucco box invasion.

Newtown Hardware House

108 S State St
Newtown, PA 18940
(215) 968-3611
www.newtownhardware.com

3

Mod Betty® Says:

✳ *Ask to see where evidence of an 1899 fire can be seen in the brick out back*

✳ *If you're lucky they may be having a craft beer sampling on a Saturday!*

✳ *Open 7 days a week, just like modern stores*

Scan the Stamp!
for map, website and additional info!

PhillyBurbs

Tag your photos from your visit
#RetroRoadmapPHILLYBURBS

Newtown Theatre
Newtown, PA

Walking past this staid brick structure on State Street you may think it is a church. Well, at one point it was one, for traveling ministers. Or perhaps you think it is a town hall? It was that too - built in 1831 as Newtown Hall, then later reconfigured in the 1880s as a place where the townspeople would gather for meetings and stage shows.

What you might not realize is that this is actually the oldest movie theater in the United States. The Newtown Theatre, with only the glow of the neon sign above the door giving a nod to its Hollywood history. They were the first theater to show movies, beginning in 1906.

With current seating for just over 350 people, the other claim to fame is that it is one of only two theaters in the Philadelphia region where you can watch a movie from the balcony.

There's little in the way of lobby space, with the exception of the ticket booth and a place to buy your popcorn and snacks. The auditorium is somewhat simple with not much in the way of ornamentation or opulent decor. Heck, air conditioning was not even installed until 2002! But the charm of watching a movie in this historic place is undeniable, especially when you can catch a silent film with live piano accompaniment.

The Newtown Theatre offers more than just movies however, bringing live theater, comedians, independent film screenings and concerts to this Bucks county borough of just over 2000 residents.

Newtown Theatre ⑨④

120 N State St
Newtown, PA 18940
(215) 968-3859
www.thenewtowntheatre.com

 Mod Betty® Says:

❋ *M. Night Shyamalan's "Signs," had it's premier here (it was partially filmed in Newtown)*

❋ *Anti-slavery meetings were held here - including an appearance by Frederick Douglass*

❋ *The other balconied theater in the area is the Colonial in Phoenixville. Mod B's hometown fave!*

Scan the Stamp!
for map, website and additional info!

PhillyBurbs

Tag your photos from your visit
#RetroRoadmapPHILLYBURBS

Date: / /

My Visit: _____

_____

_____

_____

_____

_____

_____

_____

_____

_____

_____

_____

_____

_____

_____

_____

BUCKS COUNTY

Don't forget to check it off The List!

Perkasie Carousel
Perkasie, PA

You'll have to plan your visit to the Perkasie Carousel carefully if you want to cross it off your list, as it is only open a few Sundays a YEAR. But once you get there you'll see it's a bargain, as rides are only 35 cents apiece!

This carousel, located in Menlo Park in Perkasie (PER ka-SEE) is one of the only remaining pieces from when this was the center of entertainment in the borough during the first half of the 20th century. You would never know it now, but at one point there were amusement rides, a dance hall, roller skating and even a harness race track located here.

There has been a carousel in operation here since 1892, but the current one has only been here since 1951, replacing the original carousel. This merry-go-round was made by the Herschell company, and while it is not one of the more opulent carved carousels you may be used to seeing, it is interesting in its own right.

You see, the 36 horses are actually made of metal instead of carved wood! This style of carousel was made with traveling carnivals in mind, who had to set up and break down often. Metal molded horses could be moved around without fear of chipping or breaking like wooden horses.

Since the Perkasie Historical Society took over operation in 1970 the ticket prices have only been raised a whopping 20 cents. Be nice and drop a few more dollars in the donation jar.

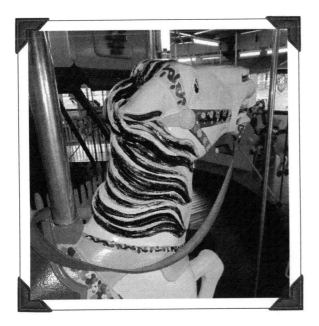

Perkasie Carousel ⑤

W Park Ave
Perkasie, PA 18944
(215) 257-5460
www.perkasiehistory.org/Carousel.htm

Mod Betty® Says:

❋ *Reasonably priced snacks and carousel inspired gift items are available–indulge and support!*

❋ *The rounding board and scenery are rare examples of a 1940's Art Deco design*

❋ *The band organ has been modernized so it can be muted it from a distance*

Scan the Stamp!
for map, website and additional info!

PhillyBurbs

Tag your photos from your visit
#RetroRoadmapPHILLYBURBS

BUCKS COUNTY

Date: / /

My Visit: _____

_____
_____
_____
_____
_____
_____
_____
_____
_____
_____
_____
_____
_____
_____
_____

Don't forget to check it off The List!

Sellersville Theater
Sellersville, PA

The Sellersville Theater hasn't been a theater since 1894, but for the past 15 years it has drawn folks to town for live music events, and was the local movie house for decades before that. Today folks come from miles around to hear Americana, Jazz, Rock and Jam Bands, Blues, R&B and more. Mod Betty has seen plenty of great shows here, and Retro Roadhusband has even graced the stage a few times himself!

The building was originally the livery stable for the Washington House next door. Throughout the years it had a variety of uses including a garage for automobiles, and was the local movie theater in town starting in 1950. Known as the SelVil, it was in operation until 1970 when a fire tore through the building.

Renamed Cinema 1894 when it reopened in 1972, it was purchased by the owners of the Washington House in 2001. Reopening in 2002, the theater was transformed into a 300 seat venue for live music, with brand new seats, completely upgraded electric and plumbing, and decorative antique sconces lining the walls.

Further improvements were made in later years including an added deck, and expanded lobby space to give more room near the snack bar. And I do mean bar, as they serve wine and beer (and snacks) before and during shows. You can bring your drinks to your seat, and if you sit in the Cabaret area your seats include a table for you to place your goodies on.

Sellersville Theater

6

24 W Temple Ave
Sellersville, PA 18960
(215) 257-5808
www.st94.com

BUCKS COUNTY

Date: / /

My Visit: _____

 Mod Betty® Says:

✳ Note the bar is cash only, but you can buy "Lobby Loot" at the box office

✳ Theater members get first dibs on the good seats, so if you're local you might want to join.

✳ Arrive early for dinner/drinks at the Washington House, that's what we do!

Scan the Stamp!
for map, website and additional info!

PhillyBurbs

Tag your photos from your visit
#RetroRoadmapPHILLYBURBS

Don't forget to check it off The List!

Sine's 5 & 10
Quakertown, PA

A 5 &10 store, opened in 1912 and still owned by the same family? YES! Sine's in Quakertown is one of Mod Betty's first PA Retro Roadmap finds, and such a fave she had to create the website just to share places like this with everyone, since they are such a rarity.

The front of the store is red and shiny just like the Woolworth store that you may remember from your youth. But it doesn't stop there - step in and wonder of wonders, there's a fully functional lunch counter, serving breakfast, lunch and ice cream treats.

The store is huge, selling all sorts of random things that made 5 and 10s so great- tricycles, styrofoam balls, dishes, dowels, hardware, candies, measuring cups, house numbers, you

name it. There is another room off to the side with notions and yarn, and a back room that has holiday decorations in it. Not only a full service store, Sine's is also an unofficial museum of retail history and vintage ephemera, courtesy of the collections of patriarch Bill Harr.

The counter, anchored on the far end by an original Hires Root Beer barrel, is the gathering place for shoppers and family members alike. From your swivel stool at the counter you'll see many generations of the Harr family hard at work. Whether cooking your breakfast or lunch, operating the cash register, or prepping the displays of the latest merchandise to arrive, this gem of a store is a family affair and a treasure for us all.

Sine's 5 & 10

7

236 W Broad St
Quakertown, PA 18951
(215) 536-6102
www.sines5and10.com

Mod Betty® Says:

❋ *Check out the display of antique cameras - what a collection!*

❋ *Look in the cooler for Moxie, if they have a bottle, try it - I dare you!*

❋ *Note, cash only at the lunch counter, but credit cards can be used to shop*

Scan the Stamp!
for map, website and additional info!

PhillyBurbs

Tag your photos from your visit
#RetroRoadmapPHILLYBURBS

BUCKS COUNTY

Date: / /

My Visit: _____

Don't forget to check it off The List!

Warner's Candies

Bensalem, PA

This family-owned candy shop may be off the beaten path (or on a well-beaten path) but the house it is housed in has been here since the 1700s! The Warner family started their candy business in a bakery in nearby Bristol, and moved their sweets business into this antique home in 1955. They added onto it a bit to accommodate their expanding business, but the low ceilings and hewn wooden beams confirm you're in an old-fashioned space.

Pulling into the gravel driveway in front of the white stuccoed house with green shutters, you'll spy wonderful hand-painted signs indicating what holiday is coming up in the candy world. Oversized molded chocolate santas and Easter bunnies might greet you depending on your calendar, but to Mod Betty every day is a perfect day for chocolates!

Step inside this old timey confection shop, and you're immediately greeted by a charmingly eclectic assortment of colonial inspired displays, wallpaper and linoleum flooring. Grab an actual old fashioned wicker basket to put your selections in.

You can see where the candy is made right through the window, and they continue to use the family recipes using nothing but fresh ingredients. Chocolate covered buttercreams are a year-round favorite, and when in season their chocolate covered blueberries and strawberries draw folks from miles around.

This is the type of place you can imagine your grandmother picking up a box of Warner's double dipped mints, to bring as a hostess gift to a game of canasta with her cronies.

Warner's Candies

3518 Bristol Pike
Bensalem, PA 19020
(215) 788-1000
www.facebook.com/
Warners-Candies-172756536097999

8

BUCKS COUNTY

Date: / /

My Visit: _____

 Mod Betty® Says:

❋ *Try their Irish Potatoes in March, they're a regional treat*

❋ *Check out the grand piano in the middle of the shop, it's not just decorative, but functional!*

❋ *They ship anywhere in the US, so send an unexpected treat to a pal for a long-distance smile*

Scan the Stamp!
for map, website and additional info!

PhillyBurbs

Tag your photos from your visit

#RetroRoadmapPHILLYBURBS

Don't forget to check it off The List!

Washington House
Hotel & Restaurant *Sellersville, PA*

In this otherwise sleepy area of Bucks County, the Borough of Sellersville has drawn visitors for decades, and the businesses on the corner of Main Street and Temple Ave are sure to appeal to Retro Roadmappers looking for a fun evening or weekend getaway.

The Washington House Restaurant is located in a 200+ year old farmhouse that has been added onto throughout the decades. The Victorian-inspired exterior you see today–with wraparound porch and 4th story tower observatory–were added in the late 1800s.

This is a perfect place for a casual snack or drink in the bar area featuring the pre-prohibition back bar and tile floor. Or for a more elegant fine dining option, ask to be seated in one of the cozy dining areas within this historic building. If you're heading to the Sellersville Theater next door, this is the place to go beforehand!

The Washington House hotel recently opened above the restaurant and offers 11 updated rooms in this historic location. The antique charm is intact, but each room also offers amenities that modern travelers have become accustomed to, including free wi-fi, marble lined bathrooms with walk-in showers, and continental breakfast served in the private lounge.

Mod Betty swoons at the sight of the Tower Suite - who wouldn't want to stay in this 3-story room with exclusive access to the 4th level observatory tower? What a view!

Washington House Hotel & Restaurant

 9

136 N Main St
Sellersville, PA 18960
(215) 257-3000
www.washingtonhouse.net

 ## Mod Betty® Says:

✳ *Story goes that the drawers behind the bar were once used by guests to store their guns!*

✳ *Legend has it the the Liberty Bell spent the night here in 1777 when being moved to hide it from the British in Philadelphia!*

✳ *Check out the WPA mural at the 1937 Post Office just next door.*

Scan the Stamp!
for map, website and additional info!

PhillyBurbs

Tag your photos from your visit
#RetroRoadmapPHILLYBURBS

BUCKS COUNTY

Date: / /

My Visit: _____

_____

_____

_____

_____

_____

_____

_____

_____

_____

_____

_____

_____

_____

_____

_____

_____

Don't forget to check it off The List!

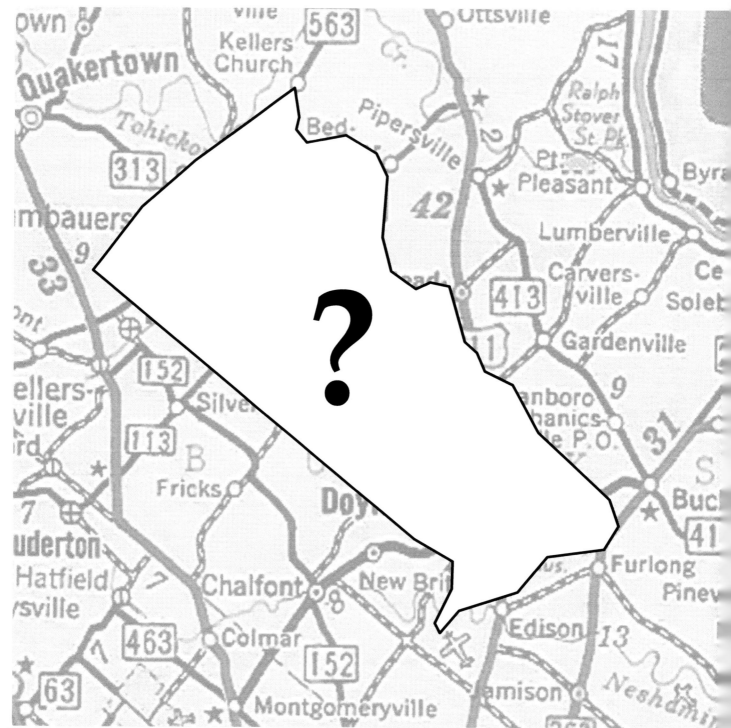

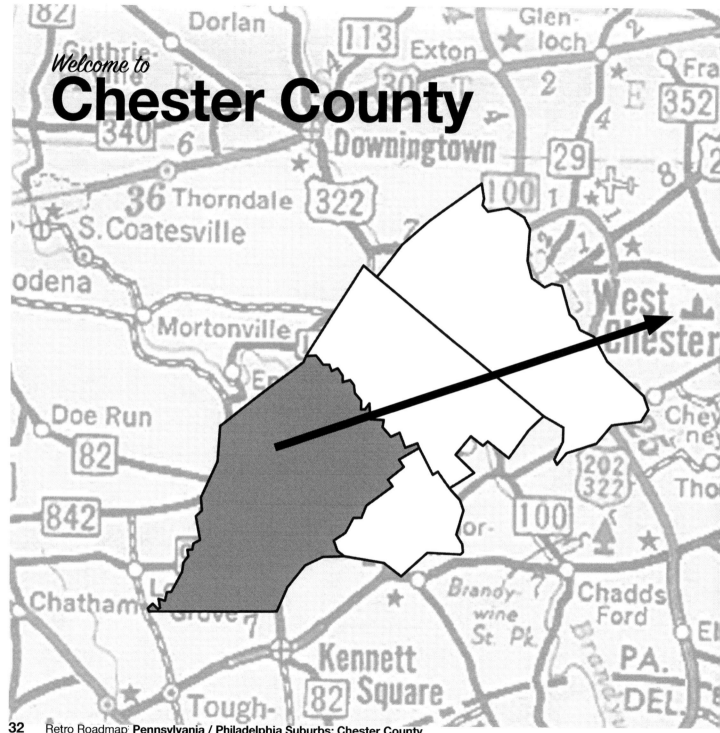

Welcome to
Chester County

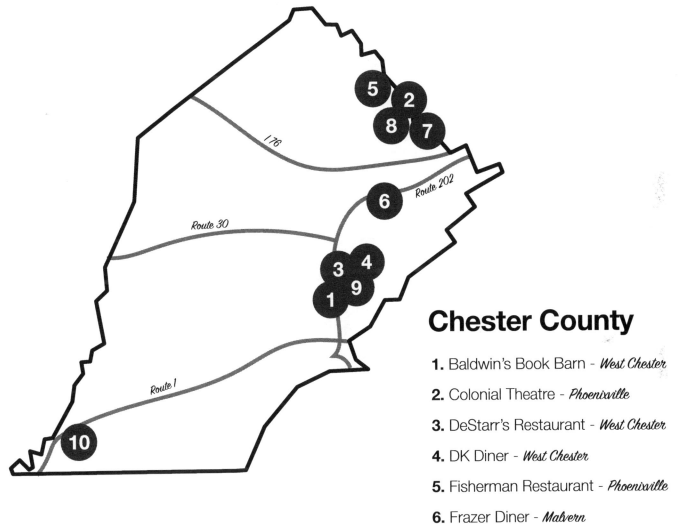

Chester County

1. Baldwin's Book Barn - *West Chester*

2. Colonial Theatre - *Phoenixville*

3. DeStarr's Restaurant - *West Chester*

4. DK Diner - *West Chester*

5. Fisherman Restaurant - *Phoenixville*

6. Frazer Diner - *Malvern*

7. G Lodge Restaurant - *Phoenixville*

8. Lulu Boutique & Gifterie - *Phoenixville*

9. Malena's Vintage Boutique - *West Chester*

10. Miss Oxford Diner - *Oxford*

Don't use this map for navigation, silly!

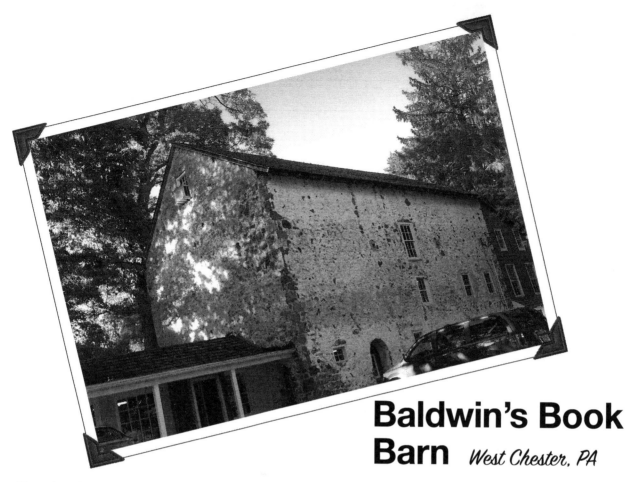

Baldwin's Book Barn *West Chester, PA*

Though only a mile outside of busy West Chester center, driving down the winding roads of the Brandywine Valley to get to Baldwin's Book Barn is also like traveling back in time. Especially when you find yourself pulling up to a stone dairy barn built in 1822!

William and Lilla Baldwin started their book selling business in 1934, moving it to this barn in 1946, and adding a living space and office in the 1950s. Their son Tom literally grew up in the business, and has run it since the 1980s.

The smell of wood smoke will greet you as soon as you enter, cluing you into the only source of heat, so dress accordingly in the winter. Shelves in this area are lined with rare and antique books, as well as more decorative "books by the yard" - popular with decorators and those who want the appearance of education without the effort.

The stone-walled barn itself is a 5 story low-ceilinged maze of shelves, nooks, steps and staircases, with over 250,000 books and prints on display, and the occasional visit from a cat or two. Antique wooden chairs scattered throughout are an understood invitation for you to settle down and peruse your selections. Books are displayed by category - grab a map and head to your favorite.

In addition to the thrill of the hunt for a long lost book, be on the lookout for the colorful vintage labels peeking out from the edges of the shelves made from vintage wooden fruit crates.

Baldwin's Book Barn  1

865 Lenape Rd
West Chester, PA 19382
(610) 696-0816
www.bookbarn.com

 Mod Betty® Says: ——

❉ *Ceilings can be low in places! Duck your head or you'll Grouse when you bump it*

❉ *Open every day except Thanksgiving, Christmas, New Years Day*

❉ *Baldwin's may be for sale to the right owner, visit sooner rather than later!*

Scan the Stamp!
for map, website and additional info

Tag your photos from your visit
#RetroRoadmapPHILLYBURBS

PhillyBurbs

Date: / /

My Visit: _____

CHESTER COUNTY

Don't forget to check it off The List!

The Colonial Theatre

Phoenixville, PA

The jewel in the crown of downtown Phoenixville, the Colonial Theatre is truly a gem. Built in 1903 it has been a movie theater, a live theater and today shows a combination of independent films, classic movies, children's programs, live music and more. Even better, it has recently expanded into the adjacent classic bank building, allowing for more lobby room and 2 more screening rooms.

The only downtown theater left in Chester County, it is noticeable for the decision in the 1999 restoration process to not go back to the original 1903 version of the facade, but instead the exterior gleams yellow. This choice echoes the 1950's-era art deco look of the theater, known locally and also internationally.

You see, this colorful facade is probably the most famous thing about the Colonial, since it is prominently featured in the 1958 horror/sci-fi/ kitsch-fest movie The Blob (starring a young Steve McQueen.) Frightened moviegoers stream frantically out of the yellow-fronted theater, with The Blob right behind them!

In addition to movies and live shows, in partnership with the Theatre Organ Society of the Delaware Valley, there are organ concerts conducted on the Wurlitzer Opus 585 theatre organ housed underneath the stage. During concerts the organ can be raised and lowered on a lift.

One of only 2 theaters left in the Philadelphia area where you can watch a movie from the balcony (the other being the Newtown Theatre) - a visit to the Colonial is a treat for all.

The Colonial Theatre 2

227 Bridge St.
Phoenixville, PA 19460
(610) 917-1228
www.thecolonialtheatre.com

Date: / /

My Visit: _____

Mod Betty® Says:

✳ *A recreation of the "Running of The Blob" scene happens at Blobfest every July!*

✳ *Historic Tours are available to go behind the scenes (Mod Betty invented 'em!)*

✳ *Don't forget to visit the balcony and rub the bronze Blob for good luck!*

Scan the Stamp!
for map, website and additional info

PhillyBurbs

Tag your photos from your visit
#RetroRoadmapPHILLYBURBS

Don't forget to check it off The List!

DeStarr's Restaurant & Bar *West Chester, PA*

Keep your eyes peeled for the sign for DeStarr's Restaurant and Bar on Gay Street in West Chester or you may miss one of the oldest Retro Roadmap-worthy places in this hip and historic borough of brick.

Started in 1935 by George DeStarr (the Americanization of his Greek name, thanks to Ellis Island) as the Gay Street Grill, current owner Bill "Vasilios" Stavropoulos is George's nephew. Bill started working at his uncle's eatery in 1951 after emigrating from Greece to the US.

Open for breakfast and lunch, if you sit at one of the vintage cantilevered stools at the counter you may be able to watch your meal be prepared on the grill in the window. However the Greek specialties, home-made soups and roasted turkey "just like Thanksgiving" are created in the kitchen in back.

Speaking of out back - don't forget to peek into the bar area to see where the first liquor license granted in town after Prohibition is still in use, or if you just want a cocktail. If you're truly inquisitive, ask Bill to see the murals of Greece painted on the dining room walls adjacent to the luncheonette area.

In a college town with so many trendy options for artisanal fare, sometimes it's a comfort to have a simple sandwich and a cup of soup sitting in one of the tufted colonial-style booths.

DeStarr's is small enough that you may find yourself easily in conversation with your fellow diners, or if you're lucky with Bill himself!

DeStarr's Restaurant ③

112 E Gay St
West Chester, PA 19380
(610) 692-4160

CHESTER COUNTY

Date: / /

My Visit: _____

_____
_____
_____
_____
_____
_____
_____
_____
_____
_____
_____
_____
_____
_____
_____
_____

Don't forget to check it off The List!

Mod Betty® Says:

❋ *Look for the day's specials listed on the board inside the restaurant*

❋ *They're known for the gyros and Greek yogurt (not together, silly!)*

❋ *Care for a hair of the dog or a nip at noon? The bar is open all day!*

Scan the Stamp!
for map, website and additional info

PhillyBurbs

Tag your photos from your visit
#RetroRoadmapPHILLYBURBS

DK Diner *West Chester, PA*

If you're not paying attention you may not realize that hidden under a green awning and picket fence "crown" the DK Diner on Gay Street in West Chester is an actual vintage diner. The business started in 1947, and the diner you see here was installed in 1953. Made by the Mountain View diner company, it was built in Singac, NJ then hauled out to West Chester.

You're greeted with the classic diner choice upon arrival - booth or counter seat? If you've got a larger crew there's an addition in the back for gathering for breakfast or lunch, 7 days a week.

The sight of classic stainless steel fan patterned backsplashes above the counter will send diner-fans hearts aflutter, and if you look closely you'll see that the open, airy feel of the diner is helped by some well placed original mirrored panels.

Traditional diner fare abounds on the menu – chicken croquettes are a Mod Betty favorite, but there is also a nod to more healthy eating with gluten-free toast and fruit salad options for breakfast. If you're there during the weekend you can choose from an expanded menu of specials including blintzes and steak and eggs.

During our visit the young staff was quick to please while engaging in conversation with customers, many of whom seem to be local. Whether refilling a cup of coffee, packing up a to-go meal or inquiring about the latest news, the DK is a place for newcomers and oldcomers alike.

DK Diner

4

609 E Gay St
West Chester, PA 19380
(610) 692-2946

www.dkdiner.com

 ## Mod Betty® Says:

✳ *Cash only but there's an ATM on-site for your convenience*

✳ *The letters D & K are thought to be for previous owners Davis & Kappy*

✳ *Open 7 days a week, the only day they're officially closed is Christmas*

Scan the Stamp!
for map, website and additional info!

Tag your photos from your visit
#RetroRoadmapPHILLYBURBS

PhillyBurbs

CHESTER COUNTY

Date: / /

My Visit: _____

_____

Don't forget to check it off The List!

The Fisherman
Phoenixville, PA

Thought you'd never know it from the outside, The Fisherman Restaurant in Phoenixville is a complete time portal. When you walk in you'll have to double check what decade it is, as so little has changed since it opened in 1960.

This small family-run restaurant is still operated by the Zaremba family (Walter and Charles.) It was opened by and named after their dad, the original "Fisherman" who would go to the Chesapeake Bay to fish, then bring his catch home to the restaurant to serve.

While fish and seafood still feature prominently (though not hand-caught), the menu also includes many standard comfort food staples - my ultimate fave being the chicken croquettes (with a side of pickled beets, please). They are also famous for

their pies, especially the strawberry, though I am usually too stuffed to get dessert.

Besides the food, the best thing ever about The Fisherman is the decor, a beautiful study in preserved materials, patterns and textures. This combination is kept tastefully in check by an overarching neutral palette, as to not overwhelm.

A visual feast from the checkered linoleum floor to the recessed ceiling with its leafy light fixtures, with the most riotous pattern I've ever seen used on the vinyl booths and counter stools. These fixtures were custom made for the restaurant by Walt and his father, so lucky for us they're not easily replaced by newly made off the rack ones. They are worth their weight in gold for that stepped-back-in-time effect.

The Fisherman ⑤

440 Schuylkill Rd
Phoenixville, PA 19460
(610) 933-7340
www.facebook.com/TheFishermanRestaurant

CHESTER COUNTY

Date: / /

My Visit: _____

_____

_____

_____

_____

_____

_____

_____

_____

_____

_____

_____

_____

_____

_____

Don't forget to check it off The List!

 ## Mod Betty® Says:

❊ *We shot a Retro Roadmap video here - check our YouTube page!*

❊ *Open for Breakfast, Lunch, Dinner but closed on Mondays*

❊ *M Night Shyamalan filmed a scene from his movie "Split" here*

Scan the Stamp!
for map, website and additional info!

PhillyBurbs

Tag your photos from your visit
#RetroRoadmapPHILLYBURBS

Frazer Diner
Malvern, PA

If you're anywhere near the Old Lincoln Highway in Chester County, you must make plans to eat at the Frazer Diner in Malvern. Don't be confused by signs for a Classic Diner, as that is not a diner, but the Frazer certainly is a classic. And a Diner.

Established in the mid 1930s, the Frazer is thought to be one of the last remaining examples of a (mostly) unaltered O'Mahony-built streamline modern diner, and you'll notice this as soon as you step inside.

With the exception of chairs and tables instead of wooden booths against the windows, there is plenty of authentic vintage diner charm to wallow in at the Frazer. Notice the marble counter, checkerboard tile floor and original counter stools still in good repair. The original wood paneling gives a warm ambiance, and the brushed stainless steel gives just a hint of what all diners would soon be made of.

Like many of the cozy diners Mod Betty is fan of, the Frazer is cash only and open just for breakfast and lunch. The menu is as small as the diner, but who needs a spiral-bound plastic tome when basic diner fare is what you're after? Tasty breakfast meats are sourced from Lancaster county or the butcher shop just up the street (Worrell's.)

Important to Note - the diner owner does not take kindly to photographs being snapped inside the diner, and you may be reprimanded if you are found doing so (Mod Betty speaks from experience-!)

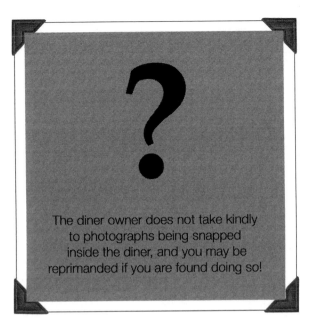

The diner owner does not take kindly to photographs being snapped inside the diner, and you may be reprimanded if you are found doing so!

Frazer Diner
189 Lancaster Ave
Malvern, PA 19355
(610) 251-9878
www.facebook.com/pages/Frazer-Diner/133504180024784

Date: / /

My Visit: _____

CHESTER COUNTY

 ## Mod Betty® Says:

✳ *Check out the fabulous O'Mahony diner clock - it still works!*

✳ *Mod Betty swoons at the thought of a slice of tomato instead of breakfast potatoes!*

✳ *Cash only so bring your money-wallet or purse*

Scan the Stamp!
for map, website and additional info!

PhillyBurbs

Tag your photos from your visit
#RetroRoadmapPHILLYBURBS

Don't forget to check it off The List!

G Lodge Restaurant
Phoenixville, PA

If you've just visited Valley Forge National Park you may still be in the Colonial-era headspace, so why not continue in that vein by breakfast/lunching at the G Lodge? The inside of this unassuming roadside eatery (attached to an auto repair shop) echoes the log cabin structures of adjacent national park, just not as drafty.

Originally opened in 1928 by Bill Gordon (hence the G in "G" Lodge) this little luncheonette has been owned for 30+ years by the Dreibelbis family, who promised not to change the name when they took ownership.

Daily specials are listed above the counter, and there's a lot on the menu as well. My eyes tend to always be bigger than my stomach here, though I've never sprung for the G-Buster special.

Unlike many diner fans I am not a fan of breakfast homefries so I love that they have potato patties (deep fried!) as an option.

We appreciate the diner-like counter seating when it is just the two of us, as the tables are cozily crammed together. We've never found the table situation a problem as most folks keep to their own personal space, but if you're one who needs plenty of elbow room, this is a heads up.

Speaking of heads, make sure not to bonk yours on the wonderful giant stone fireplace replete with Colonial-era inspired decor and hewn log mantlepiece. If you grew up in the bicentennial era you will certainly have a 1976 flashback, especially when you see the curtains!

G Lodge Restaurant

1371 Valley Forge Rd
Phoenixville, PA 19460
(610) 933-1646
www.facebook.com/
G-Lodge-125061744229855

 ## Mod Betty® Says:

✳ Cash only but ATM on-site in the front entrance

✳ The G-Lodge was The Filbert in the M-Night movie "The Happening" filmed here

✳ Breakfast is served until 1:30 every day

Scan the Stamp!
for map, website and additional info!

Tag your photos from your visit
#RetroRoadmapPHILLYBURBS

PhillyBurbs

Date: / /

My Visit: _____

CHESTER COUNTY

Don't forget to check it off The List!

Lulu Boutique & Gifterie *Phoenixville, PA*

While Lulu's isn't decades-old like many of the places Retro Roadmap loves, this little shop has done so much to put Phoenixville on the Vintage map that it would be a sin not to share it with you. Located on Main Street, you can't miss their yarn-bombed tree and eye-catching window displays.

Owned by pals Joan Moore and Keely Barone-Wrigley, the shop is a cheerful destination for ladies (and some gents) looking for wearable vintage clothing/accessories. A smattering of housewares, retro decor and kitschy collectibles are often found, depending on what treasures these two unearth during their adventures.

However, it's not only their funky storefront that will draw you to town, but the many vintage-forward events this dynamic duo have created that will have you visiting our little borough.

These gals have helped keep the fun going with parties during Phoenixville's annual Blobfest (July) and Firebird Festival (December). However the event that has put them on the map – and in magazines – is their vintage flea market known as A Whole Lot of Lulu.

Two Saturdays a year a block of Main Street and the adjacent parking lot is transformed into Whole "Lot" of Lulu - get it? Vendors of vintage, antique and handcrafted items turn the town into a unique destination for pickers and collectors of all kinds.

As you groove to tunes spun on thriftstore-found records you can shop, socialize and admire the occasional vintage camper or hot rod. Heck, you may even see Mod Betty vending this very book!

Lulu Boutique & Gifterie

12 S Main Street
Phoenixville, PA 19460
(610) 933-1852
www.awholelotoflulu.com

Mod Betty® Says:

✳ *Closed on Mondays, can't hurt to call ahead for hours to be sure other days*

✳ *Minx Vintage is their new neighbor, go say hi to Kerri too!*

✳ *Phoenixville is a cute little town (Mod Betty is biased) plan to spend a few hours here*

Scan the Stamp!
for map, website and additional info!

PhillyBurbs

Tag your photos from your visit
#RetroRoadmapPHILLYBURBS

CHESTER COUNTY

Date: / /

My Visit: _____

_____

_____

_____

_____

_____

_____

_____

_____

_____

_____

_____

_____

_____

_____

_____

_____

Don't forget to check it off The List!

Malena's Vintage Boutique *West Chester, PA*

Fans of fashion know how much fun it can be to add a bit of throwback flair into their everyday lives, from a simple brooch to an entire outfit. But bricks and mortar vintage clothing shops are becoming more and more rare, so when one has been thriving in a busy downtown location for over 10 years, Mod Betty knows that it's a place worth sharing.

Malena's Boutique has been a go-to place in the PA vintage fashion scene since opening in 2003. Occupying a corner location on West Gay Street, this sunny welcoming shop is a must-visit for folks who like to add a dash or more of unique retro style to their wardrobe for a one-of-a-kind, fashion-forward look.

Owner Malena Martinez curates the collection - each piece hand picked by herself, with eye to what is going on in the contemporary clothing scene. Her fashion background enables her to lend a friendly assist when you're trying to assemble an ensemble from frock to jewelry to handbag. This ensures that you'll feel current and not costumed, confident that you'll be wearing a one-of-a-kind look in the midst of mall copycats.

Mod B is always thrilled to see the wide selection of wearable dresses, from everyday cotton shifts to designer eveningwear - perfect for prom, rehearsal dinner or you-name-it fancy occasion. In this era of flimsy mass-market disposable clothing, vintage clothing offers the most sustainable way to stay cloaked and comfortable, with quality that will last for decades more.

Malena's Vintage Boutique

9

101 W Gay St
West Chester, PA 19380
(610) 738-9952
www.malenasboutique.com

Date: / /

My Visit: _____

CHESTER COUNTY

Mod Betty® Says:

❋ *Shopping is a breeze here with clean clothes - no musty thrift shop smells here!*

❋ *Want to stay in the loop for sales and specials? Follow Malena's on social media*

❋ *If it's not too busy in the shop, ask about the secret back room clothing stash!*

Scan the Stamp!
for map, website and additional info!

PhillyBurbs

Tag your photos from your visit
#RetroRoadmapPHILLYBURBS

Don't forget to check it off The List!

Miss Oxford Diner
Oxford, PA

Out in the countryside of southern Chester County, Retro Roadmap-worthy stops are few and far between, so the Miss Oxford diner is an oasis when you drive anywhere near Oxford. You can't miss their cheery pink and blue oversized neon sign beckoning you to come in for a meal.

A stainless steel "Silk City" diner built by the Paterson Vehicle Company of Paterson NJ, the Miss Oxford has been at this location since 1954, replacing an earlier diner at the same spot. In 1994 the diner was renovated, but lucky for us they wisely chose to highlight the original features of this classic diner, like the curved formica-covered ceiling, counter seating and stainless backsplashes.

Doing a bustling business at lunchtime, there are daily specials

as well as traditional diner faves on the menu. As you wait for your meal be delivered by the friendly waitstaff, there's plenty of vintage "ephemera" on display to entertain you. Sadly the wallbox juke boxes at the booths no longer work, but flipping through the selections is a trip to another era for sure.

Speaking of booths: before you leave the diner, take a peek at the booth closest to the far door leading to the restrooms: It's 1/2 size – just big enough for one person!

Bonus for the collector in your group, they sell their classic diner mugs emblazoned with the diner sign. Mod Betty added one to her collection to remind her to visit this diner any time she's on Route 1 just north of the Maryland line.

Miss Oxford Diner (10)

233 S 3rd St
Oxford, PA 19363
(610) 932-2653
www.missoxforddiner.com

 ## Mod Betty® Says:

✳ *Note the clock above the entrance, a rare sight on vintage diners nowadays*

✳ *They take credit cards! Another rarity in the Retro Roadmap world*

✳ *Open 7 days a week but call ahead to make sure they're open when you want to visit*

Scan the Stamp!
for map, website and additional info!

PhillyBurbs

Tag your photos from your visit
#RetroRoadmapPHILLYBURBS

Date: / /

My Visit: _____

_____

_____

_____

_____

_____

_____

_____

_____

_____

_____

_____

_____

_____

_____

_____

CHESTER COUNTY

Don't forget to check it off The List!

_____

_____

_____

_____

_____

_____

_____

_____

_____

_____

_____

_____

_____

_____

_____

_____

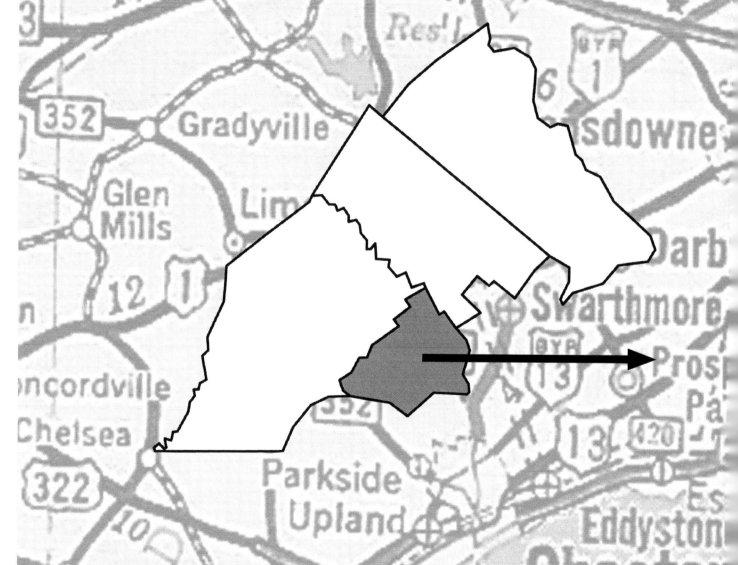

Welcome to **Delaware County**

Delaware County

1. Anthony Wayne Theater - *Wayne*

2. Booths Corner Farmers Market - *Garnet Valley*

3. Chung Sing Restaurant - *Ardmore*

4. Deals Variety Store - *Media*

5. Hungry A - *Springfield*

6. Jimmy John's - *West Chester*

7. Media Theatre - *Media*

8. Original Thunderbird - *Broomall*

9. Philadelphia Skating Club - *Ardmore*

10. R. Weinrich German Bakery - *Newtown Square*

11. Tower Theater - *Upper Darby*

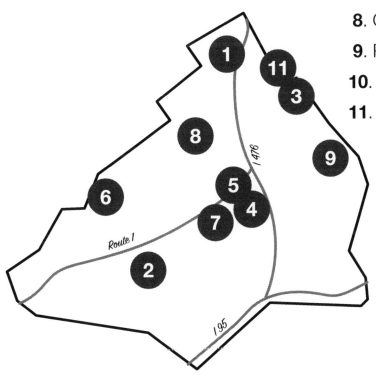

Don't use this map for navigation, silly!

Anthony Wayne Theater *Wayne, PA*

Downtown movie houses are a rarity these days, and those who have hung onto some of their authentic vintage charm are even rarer. That is why the sight of the beautiful terracotta facade and rounded marquee of the Anthony Wayne Theatre is guaranteed to put a smile on your face as you visit downtown Wayne.

The theater opened in 1928 and is located on a busy commercial stretch known as The Main Line, and Route 30, also the Lincoln Highway. Originally constructed with just one auditorium, the current space is now carved up into 5 different screening rooms. While this is never how we purists like to see vintage movie theaters treated, it is a reaction to the times to allow the theater to generate more income, when able to present five shows per night versus one.

There is still evidence of the charm that may still exist just below the dropped ceilings as you gaze above the concession stand to see the art deco details in the lobby ceiling. Also en route to screen 5 there are cutouts in the faux walls where some of the original ornate carvings are on display.

In addition to first run films, The Anthony Wayne also has a monthly Reel Cult Classics program, showing cult movies and offbeat films, as well as kids shows and matinees. We're encouraged in speaking with current management as they look to expand both programming and highlight the historic details of the theater. Fingers crossed for the AW!

Anthony Wayne Theater

109 W Lancaster Ave
Wayne, PA 19087
(610) 225-2442
www.reelcinemaspa.com

 ## Mod Betty® Says:

❊ *History tip! Both the town and the theater are named after the Revolutionary War general*

❊ *There are many restaurants in this walkable town – make a night of it!*

❊ *Psst. if you get into town early, check out the WPA mural the Post Office around the corner*

Scan the Stamp!
for map, website and additional info

PhillyBurbs

Tag your photos from your visit
#RetroRoadmapPHILLYBURBS

Date: / /

My Visit: _____

DELAWARE COUNTY

Don't forget to check it off The List!

Booths Corner Farmers Market

Garnet Valley, PA

Mod Betty admits that this long beige building may not be much to look at from the outside, but for two days a week the Booths Corner Farmers Market is bursting with a colorful collection of folks, food and fun.

Starting in the 1930s local Amish farmers would set up in a barn here to sell their bounty. Sadly the barn burned down in 1973, but the Cohen family (who still run the market today) rebuilt the this main building at the heart of the market.

Only open on Fridays and Saturdays, over 100 vendors including many Amish farmers, bakers, and butchers load their stalls with delicious foods and wares. The aisles are also thick with market goers gawking, sampling and socializing while they shop. If you're a "cooker," there are fresh meats, cheeses, vegetables, brown eggs and more for your larder, so bring a cooler for your finds.

For "eaters" like Mod Betty, there are too many ready-to eat foods to choose from. Handpies from the Amish bakery? A roast beef sandwich or catfish poboy? Some food stalls have their own seating if you order from them, but if not, take it to go and dine "a-la-car" or while you amble.

Not hungry? Plenty of collectibles, records, crafts, gifts, shoes, tubesocks, jewelry, arcade games and people watching to bide your time. Whatever brings you here, you're part of an 80+ year local tradition.

Booths Corner Farmers Market

1362 Naamans Creek Rd
Garnet Valley, PA 19060
(610) 485-0775
www.boothscorner.com

Date: / /

My Visit: _____

 Mod Betty® Says:

❋ *Rock and roller Bill Haley (Rock Around The Clock) performed here in the 1940s!*

❋ *Friday night big date night - go here for din and then Briggs Auctions across the street*

❋ *Check their website for coupons and extended holiday hours*

DELAWARE COUNTY

Don't forget to check it off The List!

Scan the Stamp!
for map, website and additional info

PhillyBurbs

Tag your photos from your visit
#RetroRoadmapPHILLYBURBS

Chung Sing
Restaurant *Ardmore, PA*

Full disclaimer – you'll find Mod Betty is not consistent in her disdain for "remuddled" diners, so even though the counter has been removed and the cuisine isn't classic American, she does have a wicked soft spot for the Chung Sing "Diner" in Ardmore.

Originally known as Dean's diner, this Fodero built diner has been a landmark on Lancaster Avenue since 1952. When Dean's closed there was thought that the diner may be trucked away to become part of a diner collection or demolished. Instead it was remodeled/muddled into the Chung Sing restaurant you see today, serving classic Americanized Chinese food.

Underneath the green faux tile roof you will still see many diner elements remaining, including some great diamond shaped stainless steel work in the vestibule and where the menu board would originally be located over the absent counter.

Speaking of menu, this is one area in which the current restaurant and original diner would align – the prices are incredibly affordable for the huge portions you get. The lunch combo including soup, fried rice, egg roll and entree is less than $6. Not sure if the wonton crisps and pickled veggies presented to each table are a Pennsylvania Chinese custom, but are nice to munch on while waiting for your meal.

Service is efficient and there's a steady stream of folks picking up takeout orders. Hope you arrived hungry, or you'll be leaving with a doggie bag of leftovers for later for sure.

Chung Sing Restaurant ③

210 Lancaster Ave
Ardmore, PA 19003
(610) 649-8115

Mod Betty® Says:

❋ There are two Fodero diner tags in the diner
- see if you can find them both

❋ If you eat enough to get to the bottom of your plate,
you'll note they're still using the same diner china,
in this China diner ;-)

❋ Free parking out back, or pay the meters in front

Scan the Stamp!
for map, website and additional info

Tag your photos from your visit
#RetroRoadmapPHILLYBURBS

PhillyBurbs

Date: / /

My Visit: _____

DELAWARE COUNTY

Don't forget to check it off The List!

Deals Variety Store
Media, PA

I was lucky enough to spend my formative years in a town that had a gigantic Woolworth variety store downtown. While "Woolies" is long gone, the vintage style variety store lives on in downtown Media, as Deals discount store (and Deals Office Store a few storefronts down State Street.)

Originally opened as a Woolworths, Deals is the last remaining 5 & 10 type variety store in Delaware County, and one of only two in the entire Philadelphia region. (see Sine's, Quakertown)

The big deal about the big Deals store is that it is just like walking into the variety stores of long ago. From the red sign to the tiled entrance with the W embedded to the antique wooden floors and tin ceiling, it's a treasure trove of retail history.

Chockablock full of practically any practical thing you could need here, plus plenty of trinkets. We've bought more than our fair share of lightbulbs, sugar shakers, plastic table cloths, candles, holiday decorations, hardware bits and candies. I'm sure there's something here you need or might need soon.

There are plenty of fun things to shop for at Deals as well, with a big selection of toys, decorations and candies for almost every holiday, greeting cards, candy, soda in glass bottles and more.

Don't forget that right down the block from the main Deals location is the Deals office / stationery annex with great prices on boxes, pads of paper, envelopes and cards. Mod Betty can't help but pick up a few postcards every time she visits!

Deals Variety Store

15 West State Street
Media, PA 19063
(610) 627-9996

www.dealsvarietystore.com

Date: / /

My Visit: _____

Don't forget to check it off The List!

 ## Mod Betty® Says:

✳ *Media has an adorable downtown area, so plan on spending time 'sploring*

✳ *Mod Betty loves the light bulb displayer - did you see it too?*

✳ *Wooden floor and tin ceilings for the win!*

Scan the Stamp!
for map, website and additional info

PhillyBurbs

Tag your photos from your visit
#RetroRoadmapPHILLYBURBS

Hungry A
Springfield, PA

You can't miss the painted wall, cheery Coke sign and red awning of the Hungry A, located right next to Sproul Lanes bowling in Springfield. This little breakfast and lunch spot was opened in 1964 by Anthony and Olga Coletta, and is now run by their son Bruce and his wife Mickey.

They'll be the ones with a friendly greeting when you first come in, with a quick rundown of their menu for first-timers (it's also posted above the grill.) Order at the counter, find a seat at the communal table "under the big top" or at one of the side counters, amidst the hodgepodge of Tastykakes and rolls. When your food is ready they will bring it to you.

While you're waiting for your food you'll have time to peruse the collection of vintage paper items originally collected and displayed on the walls by Bruce's dad. Bruce will give you the history of most of them, all you have to do is ask.

Thanks to a Hungry A frequent diner's recommendation, Mod Betty has a fave sandwich at the Hungry A: The Burgerama - with cheese. Served on an Amoroso's long roll, ground beef is chopped up instead of burger shaped, then dressed like a cheeseburger. Just a small change from a standard cheeseburger, but it makes all the difference in flavor.

Plan your arrival accordingly if you want a Burgerama, as they turn off the grill an hour before closing. But you can still get cold hoagies or sandwiches until they close.

Hungry A  **5**

755 W Sproul Rd
Springfield, PA 19064
(610) 543-9720
www.facebook.com/The-Hungry-A-330753103239

 ### Mod Betty® Says:

✳ *Want a milkshake? They'll spin one up on the vintage jade colored mixer*

✳ *All of the prints hanging up are actual antiques except for one - see if you can find it*

✳ *Closed Sundays and cash only, please*

Scan the Stamp!
for map, website and additional info

PhillyBurbs

Tag your photos from your visit
#RetroRoadmapPHILLYBURBS

Date: / /

My Visit: _____

DELAWARE COUNTY

Don't forget to check it off The List!

Jimmy John's
West Chester, PA

No, I am I not recommending a national sandwich chain that recently invaded our area, as to me there is only ONE Jimmy John's. THIS Jimmy John's "Pipin' Hot Sandwiches" has been a fixture on Wilmington Pike (202) just north of the Delaware border since 1940.

Had it not been for a tragic fire on the eve of their 70th anniversary you would still see many original features in this narrow restaurant sandwiched (tee-hee!) between the busy highway and farmland. However, the post-fire repairs and building still echo the original structure and layout, and there's plenty of vintage charm awaiting.

Known for their specially made natural casing hot dogs, these little wieners served on a club roll make quite the snap when you bite in. Not a fan of the snappy sausage? Never fear, there are other items on the menu bound to please, from burgers to chili, grilled cheese and milkshakes.

Jimmy John's is equally as famous for their electric train setup, delighting kids of all ages. The original owner Jimmy John was a train enthusiast, and current owner Roger Steward (who started working here in 1974) keeps the trains running on time.

Another tradition here that Mod Betty loves is the posting of the vintage photographs of Jimmy John's patrons throughout the decades. Though the original photos were lost to the fire, the negatives had been stored offsite, so Steward reprinted them to display once again. Plenty of history on this little sliver of land, fire be damned!

Jimmy John's ⑥

1507 Wilmington Pike
West Chester, PA 19382
(610) 459-3083
www.jimmyjohns1940.com

Mod Betty® Says:

❋ *Open 7 days a week and they serve breakfast*

❋ *Dig their dogs? Bring some home! Pack of 8 or 5lb boxes available*

❋ *Cash only, but there's an ATM on-site*

Scan the Stamp!
for map, website and additional info

PhillyBurbs

Tag your photos from your visit
#RetroRoadmapPHILLYBURBS

Date: _ / _ / _

My Visit: _____

_____
_____
_____
_____
_____
_____
_____
_____
_____
_____
_____
_____
_____
_____

DELAWARE COUNTY

Don't forget to check it off The List!

Media Theatre

Media, PA

Downtown Media is a Retro Roadmap fave because of the plethora of independent shops, restaurants and entertainment options. Located on East State Street the dazzling neon marquee of the Media Theatre can be seen as the welcoming gateway to this Delaware County destination.

The theater itself was built in 1927 to feature both vaudeville shows and movies, and was restored in 1994. Now known as the Media Theatre for the Performing Arts, it has become the go-to place for Broadway–style live stage shows, theater classes, live music and more.

From top to bottom this building reveals such a cornucopia of architectural delights, the more you look the more you'll see. If you can tear your eyes away from the gorgeous stainless steel and neon marquee that runs the entire length of this

otherwise traditional building you'll note that despite this mid-century inspired addition, the architecture itself is quite classical in nature.

Below the festoons (that's a real word, kids!) decorating the building front, the oversized divided glass windows with pointed pediments would not look out of place on many of the historic buildings in Philadelphia. The rounded ticket booth with its sleek art deco lines is a reminder of the movie theater origins of the building.

The interior auditorium - with seats for over 800 patrons is a delight, from the ornate ceiling medallion to the carved proscenium. Regardless of your familiarity with many of these architectural terms, an elegant evening of entertainment awaits you when you visit the Media Theatre.

Media Theatre

7

104 E State St
Media, PA 19063
(610) 891-0100
www.mediatheatre.org

Date: /   /

My Visit: _____

DELAWARE COUNTY

Don't forget to check it off The List!

Mod Betty® Says:

✳ *Media has a number of independent eateries in town, come early for your show and dine!*

✳ *For a truly vintage experience, take the trolley to town - SEPTA Route 101*

✳ *Check their website for the latest special events!*

Scan the Stamp!
for map, website and additional info

PhillyBurbs

Tag your photos from your visit
#RetroRoadmapPHILLYBURBS

Original Thunderbird
Broomall, PA

Conveniently located just a few minutes off of Pennsylvania's busy 476 (the "Blue Route") The Original Thunderbird "steakhouse" has been serving tasty hoagies, pizza and more since 1956. Since this is Pennsylvania, please note that the steak referred to here is as in "cheese steak" and not an Upscale Steak House.

This low slung building with stonework front and 3D letters does a bustling take-out business, so if you're pressed for time that could be the way to go. But if you have the time, there's table and counter service in this small but friendly shop. Plenty of vintage photos of the place attest to this being a local fave throughout the decades.

Still family owned and operated by 3rd generation Greco brothers, the Thunderbird name has a few possible origins. While some say it's named after the famed Ford car, a former employee informs that it is actually named after the Thunderbird Hotel in Las Vegas. You see, original owner Sam Greco and his bride honeymooned there, and had such a great time they took the name with them!

Famous for their cheesesteaks, hoagies, and other lunch/dinner fare they're also open early for breakfast. On a regional-food note, they offer "Pan Baked" pizza - also known in this Delco region as "Boston / Drexel Hill" style, with a puffier Greek-style crust. Since Mod Betty grew up eating this type of pizza in Massachusetts, she often can be found ordering a mini, and calls it simply delicious!

Original Thunderbird

2323 West Chester Pike
Broomall, PA 19008
(610) 356-8869
www.theoriginalthunderbird.com

8

Date: / /

My Visit: _____

DELAWARE COUNTY

Don't forget to check it off The List!

 Mod Betty® Says:

✳ *Take a closer look at the photos on the wall and see if you can spot the Thunderbird car*

✳ *Since you're in the Philly area, you can get cheese whiz on your steak – try it*

✳ *Do "The Continental" –this pizza comes with pepperoni, onions, sausage, peppers, my fave!*

Scan the Stamp!
for map, website and additional info

PhillyBurbs

Tag your photos from your visit
#RetroRoadmapPHILLYBURBS

Philadelphia Skating Club and Humane Society *Ardmore, PA*

Here's a cool vintage place - and it's literally cool! Tucked into in a residential section of Ardmore is the nation's oldest and largest figure skating club, the Philadelphia Skating Club and Humane Society, founded in 1861. Note - this Humane Society was created to help rescue people who fell through the ice, not animals.

Pulling up to the club itself you'll realize that despite the 19th century origins, the building itself is quite streamlined, in the art deco / moderne style, since it was built in 1938. The arched roof and glass block walls (reminiscent of stacked ice cubes!) allows the daylight to illuminate the interior, brightening up the ice with a natural glow.

While the club is owned by dues-paying members, non-members like us also are able to skate throughout the year by paying a per-session walk-on fee (call or check the online schedule). Skating skills a bit rusty? You can take ice skating lessons here as well.

The rink is also available to rent for private events, and can include use of the beautiful upper level lounge. This space is a throwback to the 1930s origins of the building, with a giant fireplace, chrome plated furniture and a wall of windows overlooking the ice. Join the legacy of skaters Dick Button and Scott Hamilton and glide along on this historic patch of ice!

Philadelphia Skating Club and Humane Society

9

220 Holland Ave
Ardmore, PA 19003
(610) 642-8700
www.pschs.org

 Mod Betty® Says:

✱ *Skates are available to rent if you don't have your own*

✱ *Ask if you can visit the upper lounge to peek at the andirons and backplate - gorgeous!*

✱ *Note there isn't a mention of hockey, so leave your stick behind when visiting here*

Scan the Stamp!
for map, website and additional info

PhillyBurbs

Tag your photos from your visit
#RetroRoadmapPHILLYBURBS

Date: / /

My Visit: _____

DELAWARE COUNTY

Don't forget to check it off The List!

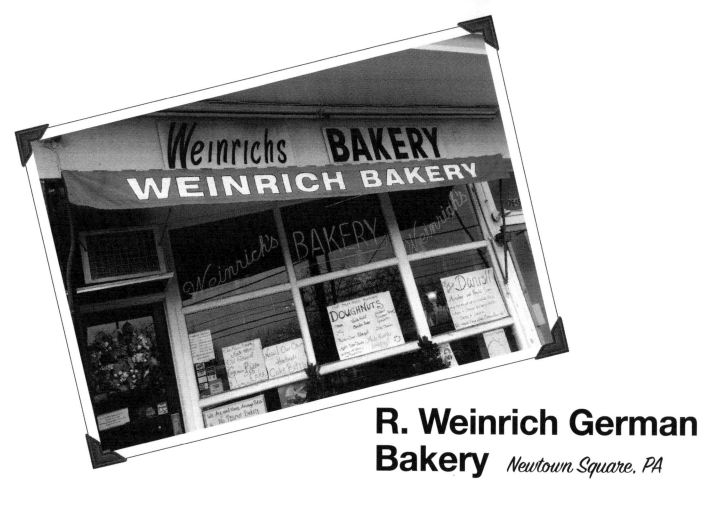

R. Weinrich German Bakery *Newtown Square, PA*

I didn't realize how rare it was to find a good old-fashioned bakery until I began looking for one. While independent bakeries are a rarity themselves, finding one that makes you feel like you've stepped back into your childhood is even more of a challenge.

Until you step into R. Weinrich German Bakery in Newtown Square, that is! The checkerboard linoleum floor, glass cases and wooden shelves haven't been replaced by newer ones. And oh, that sweet smell!

This bakery was opened in 1961 by Robert Weinrich and today the bakery is still bustling in the capable hands of his wife Marlene "Mrs. Weinrich" and their daughter Cynthia. Baking has run in the Weinrich family for over 100 years. Original-

ly from Germany, they came to Philadelphia and opened a bakery in South Philly in the 1880s.

Known for their custom cakes, cookies, pies, breads, donuts, tarts all made in the back of the store, they also offer a nice assortment of unusual items that stand out from the crowd. German butter cake, mini pastries and a unique creation known as a triangle cake (made in a triangular loaf pan.) If you're lucky you can even sample their Bavarian pretzels. Those are a lighter, airier pretzel than the traditional Philly style, and the salty snack is a great counterpoint to the sweets.

Coffee and sodas can be purchased and there are a few small tables in the window up front if you can't wait to dig in.

R. Weinrich German Bakery

3545 West Chester Pike
Newtown Square, PA 19073
(610) 356-9918
www. weinrichgermanbakery.com

10

Date: / /

My Visit: _____

_____

_____

_____

_____

_____

_____

_____

_____

_____

_____

_____

_____

_____

_____

_____

_____

DELAWARE COUNTY

Don't forget to check it off The List!

 ## Mod Betty® Says:

✺ *Closed Mondays so plan your sweet stop accordingly*

✺ *Mod Betty recommends not wearing black if you plan on eating a powdered sugar donut ;-)*

✺ *Fastnachts are a Lenten special here, try one in season!*

Scan the Stamp!
for map, website and additional info!

PhillyBurbs

Tag your photos from your visit
#RetroRoadmapPHILLYBURBS

Tower Theater
Upper Darby, PA

Music fans in the Philadelphia area and beyond know the historic Tower Theater is the place to go to for live shows, (or record a live album.) Located across the street from the 69th Street SEPTA terminal in Upper Darby, you can't miss the rounded marquee and landmark "tower atop the Tower" looming 40' above this historic theater.

Opened in 1928 as "The Aristocrat of theaters" the Tower was one of the first movie houses in the area, built by John H. McClatchy who is responsible for much of the development in the 69th Street area. (I note his name it is also the name of the of the showstoppingly-gorgeous building kitty-corner from the Tower theater, and you must take some time to ogle the decorative details.)

Like many movie/vaudeville houses, the Tower had its heyday until the second half of the 20th century. Luckily it was rescued from the jaws of death by the spirit of rock and roll, becoming a premier concert destination starting in 1972. David Bowie, Bruce Springsteen, Neil Young, Morrissey, Prince and many other big names have graced this stage over the years.

With seating for over 3000, it is one of the largest historic theaters in operation in the Philadelphia area. While some of the original opulence has been lost, concert goers can still get a thrill ascending the marble staircases to the balcony. Decorative architectural details are preserved in the main auditorium, so don't forget to appreciate them when you're rocking out!

Tower Theater

11

S 69th St & Ludlow Streets
Upper Darby, PA 19082
(610) 352-2887

www.venue.thetowerphilly.com

Date: / /

My Visit: _____

DELAWARE COUNTY

Don't forget to check it off The List!

Mod Betty® Says:

* *Pop into H&M to see the 3 story stained glass window at the McClatchy building.*

* *Now booked by LiveNation, they offer a VIP service if you're feeling fancy*

* *Easily accessible via Market - Frankford line if you don't feel like driving!*

Scan the Stamp!
for map, website and additional info

PhillyBurbs

Tag your photos from your visit
#RetroRoadmapPHILLYBURBS

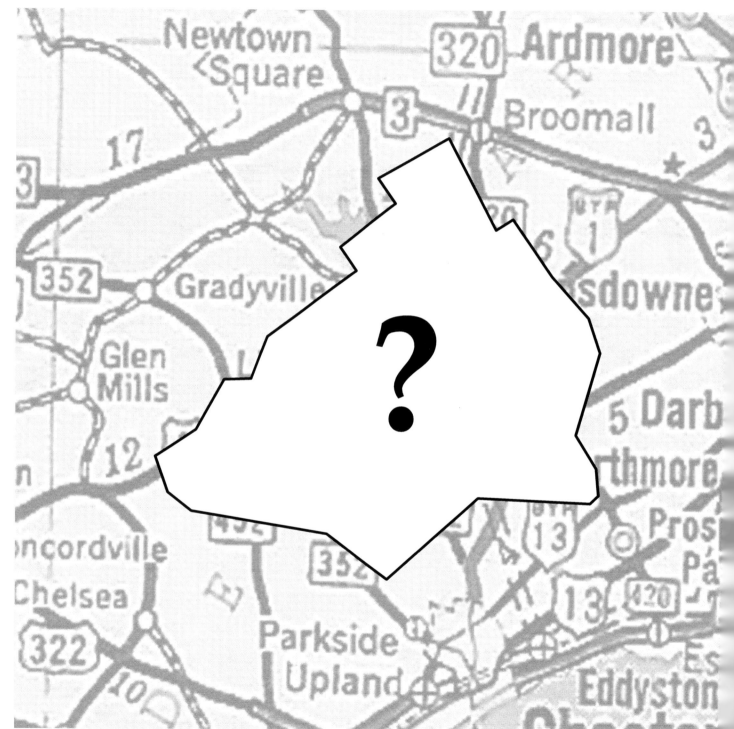

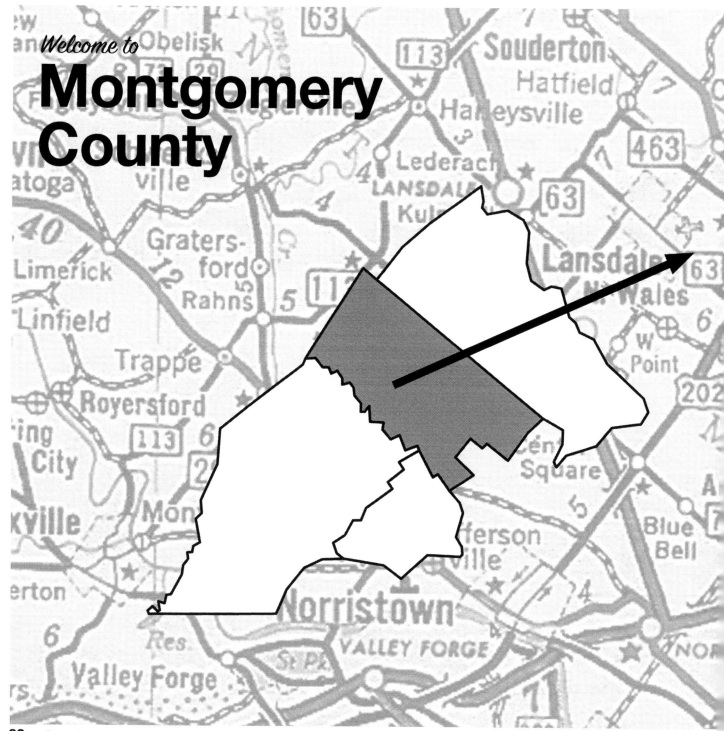

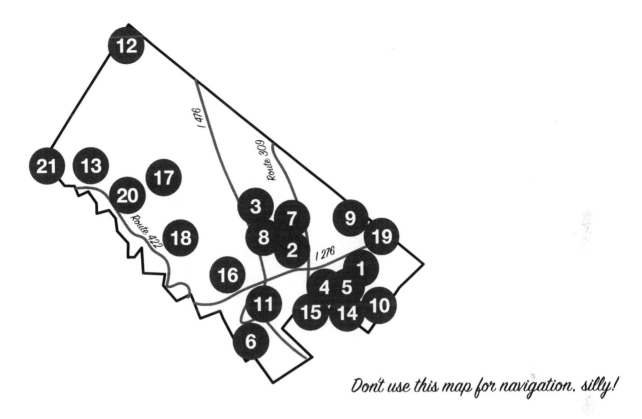

Don't use this map for navigation, silly!

Montgomery County

1. Abington Pharmacy & Gift - *Abington*

2. Ambler Theater - *Ambler*

3. Bergin's Chocolates - *Lansdale*

4. Beth Sholom Synagogue - *Elkins Park*

5. Blue Comet Bar & Grill - *Glenside*

6. Bryn Mawr Film Institute - *Bryn Mawr*

7. Burdick's Hatboro News Agency - *Hatboro*

8. Costa Deli - *Ambler*

9. Daddypops Diner - *Hatboro*

10. Danish Bakers - *Rockledge*

11. Edwards Freeman Nuts - *Conshohocken*

12. Grand Theater - *East Greenville*

13. Hill Top Drive-In Restaurant - *Pottstown*

14. Hiway Theater - *Jenkintown*

15. Keswick Theatre - *Glenside*

16. Lou's Sandwich Shop - *Norristown*

Abington Pharmacy & Gift
Abington, PA

Driving down Old York Road (Route 611) in Abington, the unique and distinctive sign for Abington Pharmacy & Gift is a cheery landmark. The neon-edged blocks noting not only that it is a Drug Store but they have Cards and Gifts, a swoop of red and a yellow lantern lighting the way reminds us to visit this family-owned shop instead of the boring chain stores surrounding it.

Opened in 1958, you could almost tell that from the low slung slope of the roof and the sign on the stonework front. It is especially beautiful to see at night when it is backlit with a pink neon glow. Inside while ogling the 50s era signage around the prescription department you might be surprised to find a still-working stamp machine.

You can visit here 7 days a week - 'til midnight no less! And while they do fill prescriptions, they offer so much more than that. Plenty of snacks - both sweet and salty - are available, as well as paperback books, stationery, toiletries, puzzles, magazines and more. A wide selection of greeting cards and gifts make this an easy place to pop into for a last minute thank you or hostess gift. They offer free gift wrapping, too.

We all know that finding a place that is holding its own against the "chainification" of the busy roadsides is a rarity. So if you're anywhere in the area, stop by - you know they'll be open, and let's do our part to keep it that way.

Abington Pharmacy & Gift

1460 Old York Rd
Abington, PA 19001
(215) 884-2767
www.abingtonpharmacypa.com

1

 Mod Betty® Says:

✳ *Remember Barton's Almond Kisses?
They sell them here!*

✳ *Make sure to tell them you are here shopping
because of their well kept vintage charm.
Positive reinforcement!*

✳ *Buy a lottery ticket here. If you win, they get
a bit of cash, too! It's a Mod Betty tradition*

Scan the Stamp!
for map, website and additional info!

PhillyBurbs

Tag your photos from your visit
#RetroRoadmapPHILLYBURBS

Date: / /

My Visit: _____

MONTGOMERY COUNTY

Don't forget to check it off The List!

Ambler Theater

Ambler, PA

The 30-foot vertical sign for the Ambler Theater is one of many delightful sights you'll see when visiting this historic destination on Butler Ave. The Spanish Colonial exterior, with matching towers, ornate terracotta designs and brickwork enveloping the two adjacent storefronts lends an international flair to the main drag in quaint downtown Ambler.

Opened in 1928 as a single screen movie house with seats for more than 1200 people, the Ambler had its heyday. But as the years passed it - like so many downtown theaters - could not survive the onslaught of TV and the ease of parking at mall movie theaters. For almost three decades is stayed open a Christian movie theater, but eventually went dark from 1997-2001.

Lucky for us and the residents of this Montgomery County community, the Ambler has since been reopened and reinvigorated by non-profit ownership. While the main auditorium has been divided into three screening rooms this enables a variety of shows to be featured simultaneously, making it a destination for first-run art and independent movies, children's programming and special events.

Millions of dollars have been invested into the theater, for structural improvements and to save as much original vintage detail as possible. Note the original tilework in the lobby, and make sure you visit the main auditorium to see the faux wood ceiling beams and gilded organ grills. And as you leave the theater, gaze downward at the stars in the sidewalk and thank the folks named there for lighting up this gem again.

Ambler Theater ②

108 E Butler Ave
Ambler, PA 19002
(215) 345-7855

www.amblertheater.org

Date: / /

My Visit: _____

_____
_____
_____
_____
_____
_____
_____
_____
_____
_____
_____
_____
_____
_____
_____
_____
_____

MONTGOMERY COUNTY

Don't forget to check it off The List!

Mod Betty® Says:

❋ *The blade sign and marquees are replicas of the originals destroyed in the 1960s.*

❋ *Become a member here and enjoy discounts at the County and Hiway, too!*

❋ *Mod Betty digs the signs above the ladies and men's rooms- do you?*

Scan the Stamp!

for map, website and additional info!

PhillyBurbs

Tag your photos from your visit

#RetroRoadmapPHILLYBURBS

Bergin's Chocolates
Lansdale, PA

I'd've been caught by the witch like Hansel and Gretel since I eagerly pulled my car into what looked like someone's home driveway, simply because there was a sign out front indicating candy ahead! But lucky for all of us, instead I found Bergin's Chocolate and candy shop.

This family run business started in the kitchen of this house in 1935 and is open year-round every day except Sundays and holidays.

If the neon Open sign is glowing in the back building come on in. You'll most likely find one of the Bergin family ready to help you. Behind the counter is where the chocolates have been made since 1940 when the business expanded out of their home kitchen and into this simple white structure behind the house.

Mike Snyder, whose grandparents started the business, notes that they use much of the same vintage machinery to mix and cool their candies, including giant copper kettles and marble slabs. They use only the best chocolate for their dipped and molded candies, and ensure everything is fresh.

Famous for their buttercreams and chocolate covered pretzels, the small shop can be bustling during the holidays. For those of you who are not fans of chocolate (rumor has it there are some of you out there-!) they offer a variety of fruit flavored pectin-based candies. Even if you can't have a piece of candy at all, stop in and buy a greeting card! You'll be happy you supported this decades old family business.

Bergin's Chocolates 3

2634 Morris Rd
Lansdale, PA 19446
(215) 699-3420
www.berginschocolate.com

 Mod Betty® Says:

❋ *Remember to bring an iced cooler in the warm months - chocolate melts in hot cars!*

❋ *There's a picnic table outside if you want to enjoy your sweets immediately*

❋ *They've got a Facebook and Yelp page, show 'em some online appreciation*

Scan the Stamp!
for map, website and additional info!

Tag your photos from your visit
#RetroRoadmapPHILLYBURBS

PhillyBurbs

Date: / /

My Visit:

MONTGOMERY COUNTY

Don't forget to check it off The List!

Beth Sholom Synagogue *Elkins Park, PA*

While there are many mid-century modern houses of worship that may have Mod Betty do a double-take when driving by, nothing makes her slam on the brakes like the sight of the Beth Sholom Synagogue in Elkins Park.

In addition to being one of the most unusual looking edifices in the area, it is the only synagogue in the world designed by the famous American architect Frank Lloyd Wright.

Lucky for us all, not only can you ogle this building from the outside, but they offers guided tours of this national historic landmark, as long as you schedule in advance. Nothing beats experiencing this space first-hand, to get a feel for what the architect was trying to accomplish with each design decision. What may seem random on first glance can often be revealed to be well thought out choice.

On your tour you will learn the history of the congregation, and why they came to Elkins Park in 1951. How in 1953 Rabbi Mortimer J. Cohen wrote to FLW (now in his mid-80s) and inspired him to accept the commission to create this unique house of worship. The building was finished in 1959 but sadly, Mr. Wright passed away a few months prior to that and never saw it completed.

While you may not think of yourself as a fan of modern architecture, you may reconsider this once you tour this building. And if not, at least you'll have a better understanding of how this grand building came to be!

Beth Sholom Synagogue

8231 Old York Rd
Elkins Park, PA 19027
(215) 887-1342

www.bethsholompreservation.org

Date: / /

My Visit:

 **Mod Betty® Says:**

✳ *In 2007 became a national historic landmark*

✳ *Look for the red square with FLWs initials in it!*

✳ *FYI - Beth Sholom is Hebrew for House of Peace. Mod Betty is also a Beth and didn't know that!*

Scan the Stamp!
for map, website and additional info!

Tag your photos from your visit
#RetroRoadmapPHILLYBURBS

PhillyBurbs

MONTGOMERY COUNTY

Don't forget to check it off The List!

Blue Comet
Bar & Grill *Glenside, PA*

The Blue Comet is one of those "new" places that Mod Betty loves, because it is Old At Heart. Though only 20 years old, you would not believe it from the throwback scene that greets you on the other side of the reeded glass door.

Classic easy listening tunes fill the air, as bartenders dressed in crisp white shirts expertly craft cocktails while chatting with patrons lining the vintage bar. Seated at the bar waiting for your drink or nibble, entertain yourself by gazing upward to try to pick out your favorite piece of vintage kitsch from the collection displayed above. Or, as the sign once said you can go old-school and "Talk To The Person Next To You."

While the Blue Comet is a bar, it is also a grill, and if you like you can sink into an upholstered booths in the dining area for a meal. The menu is heavy on American comfort foods done up right, including their infamous peanut butter bacon burger. The flickering candles atop the tables may need to be used as auxiliary light for old eyes to glance at the details on the menu, but that's just because the ambient light is kept low enough for everyone to look young and glamorous.

During the warmer weather there is seating in the back courtyard, replete with trickling fountain. Perhaps drop three coins in the fountain, and wonder which one will the fountain bless? Sinatra would approve of that, and the Blue Comet.

Blue Comet Bar & Grill

106 S Easton Rd
Glenside, PA 19038
(215) 572-9780
www.facebook.com/bluecometbar

5

 **Mod Betty® Says:**

❋ Open for lunch and still as charming during the daytime, you may not want to leave

❋ Note that this is not a place to bring the kids, it's a grown-ups only place - dress nice.

❋ Tell 'em Mod Betty sent you and you might get to visit the collection in the basement!

Scan the Stamp!
for map, website and additional info!

PhillyBurbs

Tag your photos from your visit
#RetroRoadmapPHILLYBURBS

Date: / /

My Visit: _____

MONTGOMERY COUNTY

Don't forget to check it off The List!

Bryn Mawr Film Institute *Bryn Mawr, PA*

Back in the 1920s there were a number of movie theaters along the Main Line, but now there's only one remaining that is on the National Register of Historic Places - the Bryn Mawr Film Institute.

Opened in 1926 as a movie house known as the Seville, the original neo-classical elements of the exterior are still visible: Pilasters topped with eagles, medallions with winged horses, and a symmetrical green marble-lined entryway. The marquee, while new, is a replica of the original design, and once underneath you'll enter the theater via an arched two-story glass atrium.

As with many neighborhood movie houses, the Bryn Mawr had its slow decline through the later decades, with its lowest point being threatened with closure and possible future as a gym (similar to the fate of the neighboring Ardmore Theater.)

However, a group of local residents and businesspeople saw value in maintaining the theater as a creative spot and created the Bryn Mawr Film Institute to save it. The organization purchased the building in 2004 and throughout the next 10 years renovated and expanded it to include 4 state-of-the-art auditoriums, stadium seating and large format screens.

Not only a place to see movies, the Institute is a place to learn about them, with a curriculum of film courses, in-house film education department, discussion groups and special events. The wide selection of independent, international and contemporary films to choose from (both digital and 35mm) ensure's that there's something for everyone here at this creative gathering spot.

Bryn Mawr Film Institute

6

824 Lancaster Ave
Bryn Mawr, PA 19010
(610) 527-9898
www.brynmawrfilm.org

Date: / /

My Visit:

MONTGOMERY COUNTY

Don't forget to check it off The List!

Mod Betty® Says:

❋ *Film purists will enjoy the fact that the theater is 35mm equipped along with digital.*

❋ *Mod Betty loves that they hosts the Secret Cinema screenings of vintage 16mm films here!*

❋ *Parent with infants will appreciate the Kids Matinee screenings - babies welcome*

Scan the Stamp!
for map, website and additional info!

PhillyBurbs

Tag your photos from your visit
#RetroRoadmapPHILLYBURBS

Burdick's Hatboro News Agency *Hatboro, PA*

Burdick's News Agency in Hatboro is a step back in time with something for everyone in the family. The Burdick family has owned and operated this shop since 1950, though the building itself was built in the 1860s. You can't miss the cheery yellow building with the arched barrel roof as you drive down the main thoroughfare in town.

Open every morning at 7:30am, I can imagine The Three Bears entering and immediately making a beeline to the aisle of their choice. Which bear might you be?

Papa Bear would check out the imported cigars, pipes and tobacco. After perusing those manly delights he might stop at the register for a lottery ticket or the local newspaper.

Baby Bear would go no further than a few steps in the door.

Here she would be caught between two happy places: To her right, the soda fountain, with antique swivel stools and menu offering milkshakes, ice cream sodas and sundaes. To her left there are shelves laden with candies of all sorts - many common names, but also plenty of vintage inspired ones including Necco Wafers, Dots and Clark Bars.

Mama Bear would head towards the back past the register to peruse the latest magazines, glance at the Harlequin-esque romance novels, or perhaps pick up a greeting card from the selection in the back.

So even though you're not a bear (or are you?) I bet there's something you're going to find for yourself when you go to Burdick's.

Burdick's Hatboro News Agency

7

206 S York Rd
Hatboro, PA 19040
(215) 675-9960
www.burdickstobaccoandnewshatboropa.com

Date: / /

My Visit: _____

_____

_____

_____

_____

_____

_____

_____

_____

_____

_____

_____

_____

_____

_____

_____

_____

_____

MONTGOMERY COUNTY

Don't forget to check it off The List!

 ## Mod Betty® Says:

✳ *Psst. There's parking in back of the building*

✳ *Walk through downtown Hatboro and visit the independent businesses that still exist!*

✳ *Don't forget to tune into WRDV-FM 89.3 to listen to big band, jazz and swing – they're located in downtown Hatboro!*

Scan the Stamp!
for map, website and additional info!

PhillyBurbs

Tag your photos from your visit
#RetroRoadmapPHILLYBURBS

Costa Deli *Ambler, PA*

Discovering Retro Roadmap-worthy places requires a sharp eye for detail and clues ala Nancy Drew. So when Mod Betty spotted the vintage-looking Breyers Ice Cream sign with the phrase "Hand Dipped Bulk" she thought this place might be a contender. Once she stepped inside and met owner David Costa, she knew she was right! David's grandfather from Italy opened this Ambler deli in 1950, and it is still a family run business.

While this is called a deli, there's also a counter with 5 stools, and booth and table seating too. Not only does Costa's serve the well advertised Breyers Ice Cream, they also make all sorts of hoagies, burgers, sandwiches, soups, hot dogs, homemade salads and breakfast sandwiches. They serve Levi's hot dogs which are a Philadelphia tradition.

Adjacent to the table area you'll see a large selection of imported Italian pastas sauces and olive oils. David stocks these items to save his customers a trip into Philadelphia's Italian Market. In the refrigerated section you'll also spy quality DiBruno's cheeses and Talluto's pasta.

While waiting for your food, test your skill at a game of pinball or Ms. Pacman, or take a look at the photos lining the walls, reflecting the history of the family and the business. You'll also see some signs with great prices on them. These are vintage signs and items David's dad saved, and they're on display reminding folks that Costa's has been around a long time. And we hope it stays that way!

Costa Deli

8

901 E Butler Pike
Ambler, PA 19002
(215) 646-6173
www.costadeli.net

 ## Mod Betty® Says:

✱ *Don't forget to try one of Gina's Amazing Gourmet Cupcakes!*

✱ *Did you know that Breyer logo isn't a mint leaf but a briar leaf? Makes sense!*

✱ *There's parking accessible from either side of the building*

Scan the Stamp!
for map, website and additional info!

PhillyBurbs

Tag your photos from your visit
#RetroRoadmapPHILLYBURBS

Date: / /

My Visit: _____

_____
_____
_____
_____
_____
_____
_____
_____
_____
_____
_____
_____
_____
_____
_____
_____
_____
_____

MONTGOMERY COUNTY

Don't forget to check it off The List!

Daddypops Diner
Hatboro, PA

Daddypops may be in Pennsylvania, but to Mod Betty it is like a visit back home to a favorite New England diner. Though built in New Jersey its 1953 birth-year means it is a human-scale diner seating about 60, not one of those huge diner/restaurant combos.

The diner has been a Hatboro fixture since that year, but it has been owned for the past 30 years by Ken Smith, who bought the diner in 1987 (along with his wife, Beth, who has since passed.) Ken is from New England which is perhaps why there are so many details familiar to Mod B. The "Only Open for Breakfast and Lunch" hours, and the "baked beans as a breakfast side" are two things that just scream home.

Though the diner is classic stainless steel on the outside, the inside it is a bit more rustic, with wood panels, booths and counter stools. This is softened a bit with a touch of wallpaper towards the ceiling and green gingham curtains. The mirrored wall in front of the Seeburg jukebox gives the small diner a more open feeling too. Speaking of the jukebox, you can entertain yourself by noticing all of the vintage ephemera decorating the diner, including two vintage barber chairs that double as corner counter seats!

Look for the Retro Roadmap mug along with the locals in the coffee nook, and feel free to use it! It's for all Retro Roadmappers to feel at home visiting this classic diner.

Daddypops Diner

 9

232 N York Rd
Hatboro, PA 19040
(215) 675-9717
www.facebook.com/pages/Daddy-
pops/105035539539355

 ## Mod Betty® Says:

✳ *Baked beans on toast is Mod Betty's go-to breakfast here - give it a try!*

✳ *Look for the folding paper diner atop the jukebox - it was used as a promotional piece for a drug company!*

✳ *Don't forget to tune into WRDV-FM 89.3 to listen to big band, jazz and swing - they're located in downtown Hatboro!*

Scan the Stamp!
for map, website and additional info!

PhillyBurbs

Tag your photos from your visit
#RetroRoadmapPHILLYBURBS

Date: / /

My Visit: _____

_____
_____
_____
_____
_____
_____
_____
_____
_____
_____
_____
_____
_____
_____
_____
_____
_____
_____

MONTGOMERY COUNTY

Don't forget to check it off The List!

Danish Bakers
Rockledge, PA

If every neighborhood had a local bakery as good as Danish Bakers in Rockledge, we'd all be a lot happier...and heavier! Founded in 1960 by Ray McCrimmon senior, it is still run by two generations of the McCrimmon family.

Jeweltone Tiffany-style chandeliers hang in front of an antique dough trough table, and donuts are displayed on antique wooden shelving saved from a closed Philadelphia bakery. The pot-belly stove near the entrance is a customer fave. But for all the authentic vintage touches in place since the early 1960s, the even better news is that their baked goods are as out-of-this-world tasty as they are varied.

From simple melt-in-your mouth donuts (made daily) and cinnamon buns to their award-winning Japanese jelly roll and wildly popular butter cake - a must-try Philadelphia treat.

All of the fillings for their pies and danishes are scratch-made, from lemon to fresh peach cake toppings, and Italian plums and dates for the daintily named Princess date nut bars. Breads, rolls (snowflake, onion) tea biscuits and newly introduced old fashioned pretzels are available should your sweet tooth needs a break.

Stalwart customers look forward to visiting the shop for their holiday treats from Christmas springerle, stollen and pfeffernusse to Thanksgiving pies, Lenten fastnachts and hot crossed buns.

The shop is closed every Monday, Tuesday, all of August and half of January, so plan your visit accordingly. Hopefully these breaks allow us all to lose the pounds we've of course gained from visiting Danish Bakers far too often!

Danish Bakers 10

107 Huntingdon Pike
Rockledge, PA 19046
(215) 663-9900
www.danishbakers.com

Date: / /

My Visit:

 Mod Betty® Says:

✸ Note, the family is not from Denmark - "danish" refers to the pastry

✸ They're cash only, so bring your wallet not your card

✸ You're right near Hollywood, PA - check out their lil haciendas!

MONTGOMERY COUNTY

Don't forget to check it off The List!

Scan the Stamp!
for map, website and additional info!

PhillyBurbs

Tag your photos from your visit
#RetroRoadmapPHILLYBURBS

Edwards Freeman Nut Company *Conshohocken, PA*

Edwards Freeman Nut Company (and candy mecca) is located a bit off the beaten track, but once you know where it is your sweet tooth will guide you there forevermore. The company store has been hidden at this Hector street location surrounded by residential row homes since 1959.

There is a heavy nut presence here, as the company continues to roast nuts on-site and make their own peanut butter and other nut butters. Available in smooth or crunchy, these protein-packed butters are fresh and flavorful, and a nice change from the supermarket versions.

But while many go nuts for their nuts, what is most amazing is their huge selection of candy! Aisles are lined with cubbies filled top to bottom with a wide variety of chocolates,

pectin-based candies, hard candy, fruit flavored treats, holiday items and ice cream toppings, from all over the world, and almost every decade. Wandering around Edwards Freeman is a bit like a trip back in time especially when you spy the treats of your youth, from Air Heads to Zagnut.

Savory items available here include coffees, seasonings, spices, hot sauces and drink mixes - perfect for putting into a gift basket, which they are more than happy to make up for you. Or just pick up a basket and start adding your faves to it.

A wide variety of unusual and individually priced candy bars line the checkout area, so even if you're picking up a gift, you can treat yourself to a little treat too!

Entrance

Edwards Freeman Nut Company

441 E Hector St
Conshohocken, PA 19428
(610) 828-7440
www.edwardsfreeman.com

Mod Betty® Says:

✳ Groups of 10 or more can take a tour and watch peanut butter being made - just call!

✳ The upper floors of the building used to be the factory, now they're offices

✳ Open 7 days, so no excuse not to stop by any time

Scan the Stamp!
for map, website and additional info!

PhillyBurbs

Tag your photos from your visit
#RetroRoadmapPHILLYBURBS

Date: /   /

My Visit: _____

_____

_____

_____

_____

_____

_____

_____

_____

_____

_____

_____

_____

_____

_____

_____

_____

MONTGOMERY COUNTY

Don't forget to check it off The List!

Grand Theater
East Greenville, PA

Located in the uppermost corner of Montgomery county (and closer to Allentown than Philadelphia) the Grand Theater is a gem in East Greenville, thanks to the vision of owner Ed Buchinski.

The theater was built in 1924, and when Ed purchased it in 2004 the place was a mess, to put it mildly. Fast forward to today and you'd be hard pressed to believe that the "before" photos of this theater are actually of the same location. With a lot of hard work and dedication, the theater gleams!

The auditorium's ceiling is decorative tin that replicates the original pattern. Historic elements on the walls were uncovered during reconstruction and replicated and refinished, and new seats (almost 350) have been installed. A new marquee was also created, to be visible from the street.

Concentrating mainly on family-friendly films, the Grand is a place where you can bring the entire clan and not break the bank, with ticket prices currently topping out at $5. Snacks at the reconstructed snackbar are just as value-priced, and you'll positively swoon over the gorgeous 1948 Manley popcorn popper in use.

As an extra touch of class, Ed and his staff don jackets and ties when working the theater, much like fellow theater owner Rick Wolfe and his staff at the Roxy in Northampton.

The theater has TWO organs, originally saved from other movie houses. If you're lucky you may hear them played prior to films, or during the Silent Film Series that runs each fall.

Grand Theater

12

252 Main St
East Greenville, PA 18041
(215) 679-4300
www.thegrandtheater.org

 **Mod Betty® Says:**

✳ As Ed says, and Mod Betty attests "1924 never looked so good!"

✳ The small balcony was once the smoking area

✳ Check out the deco lighting and ceiling of the Subway next door, that's Ed's doing, too!

Scan the Stamp!
for map, website and additional info!

Tag your photos from your visit
#RetroRoadmapPHILLYBURBS

PhillyBurbs

Date: / /

My Visit: _____

MONTGOMERY COUNTY

Don't forget to check it off The List!

Hill Top Drive-In Restaurant *Pottstown, PA*

The official name of The Hill Top is the Hill Top Drive-In, but nowadays there is indoor seating and you just "drive-in" to the parking spaces out front. Originally opened in 1952 as a Carvel ice cream shop, it became the Hilltop just 6 years later.

Conveniently located just a turn or two off of busy Route 422, the 2 story pink neon sign acts like a magnet to pull you in for a quick fast-food type bite, or a sweet ice cream treat. Speaking of ice cream, notice the big swirl-top ice cream cone on the roof, harkening back to the Carvel days. Today I'm happy to report they sell local Nelson's ice cream in addition to soft serve.

The interior decor is vintage knotty pine paneling, with some updated touches like the 80's retro pink/aqua "50's" color scheme, with boomerang Formica on the tables. Pick a place to order at the counter, and they'll call you when your tray is ready. You can while away the moments by looking at the vintage photos of the restaurant displayed throughout the small dining area.

Open for breakfast, lunch and dinner, the menu is more varied than a chain restaurant, with sandwiches, soups, daily specials and Mod Betty's fave - Broasted chicken. Their inexpensive burgers are on the small side (for that price they should be) but provide a quick snack for those on the go. Good's potato chips (another Mod B fave) are also offered, and their lardy goodness is addictive.

Hill Top Drive-In Restaurant

2910 E High St
Pottstown, PA 19464
(610) 326-2342
www.hilltopdrivein.com

13

 ## Mod Betty® Says:

✳ *During the warm weather they do classic car nights - check the website for dates!*

✳ *Closed Tuesdays like many old-fashioned burger joints*

✳ *Their potato puffs are what some of us refer to as tater tots*

Scan the Stamp!
for map, website and additional info!

Tag your photos from your visit
#RetroRoadmapPHILLYBURBS

PhillyBurbs

Date: / /

My Visit: _____

MONTGOMERY COUNTY

Don't forget to check it off The List!

Hiway Theater

Jenkintown, PA

This theater located at 212 York Road was built in 1913 and has had a number of name changes and incarnations in the 100+ years it has been livening up Jenkintown.

First known as the Jenkintown Auditorium and later as The Embassy Theatre, York Road Theatre, the Chas III and The Merlin Theatre (You'll spy a scrolled "M" for Merlin etched in the glass of the entry doors still) it was originally named the Hiway in 1940, and when the theater was brought under the direction of a local non-profit in 2003, the decision was made to return to the name Hiway.

Make sense to me considering how busy this stretch of road is - just try to take a photo without a car in it and you'll be snapping photos for a while - trust me!

But don't let this bustling activity discourage you from visiting this little local art-house. While it only has a single screen, they make the most of their programming, including independent, art-house, foreign films, classics (Mod Betty is a sucker for classics on the big screen) and more.

Once you enter the auditorium you'll note that seating (330) has been updated and includes two loveseat seats! If you want to snuggle with your honey or simply sprawl out yourself get there early to snag one of those coveted couches.

The 2011 replica of their original tower sign paired with the fabulous General Electric sign of Jenkintown Electric gives some well needed Hollywood glamour to the Montco 'burbs.

Hiway Theater 14

212 York Road
Jenkintown, PA 19046
(267) 864-0065
www.hiwaytheater.org

 Mod Betty® Says:

❋ *In the same family as the Ambler and County - become a member and save at all of 'em!*

❋ *Note the decorative panel above the archways leading into the auditorium*

❋ *If no one is in the ticket booth, go up to the concession stand to get your tix*

Scan the Stamp!
for map, website and additional info!

PhillyBurbs

Tag your photos from your visit
#RetroRoadmapPHILLYBURBS

Date: / /

My Visit: _____

MONTGOMERY COUNTY

Don't forget to check it off The List!

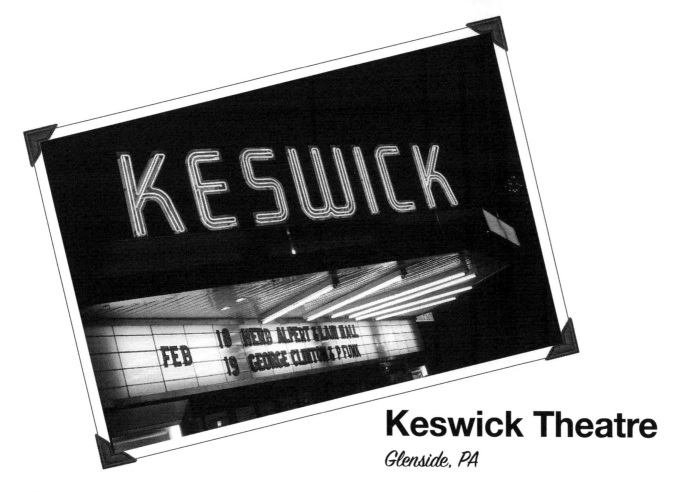

Keswick Theatre

Glenside, PA

Originally opened on Christmas night 1928 as a combination vaudeville/movie house, the Keswick Theatre is nestled in a little English village setting in Glenside. During its history it has had the ups and downs of many theaters, closing, slated for demolition, rescued and reopened. Lucky for us it has been continuously open for good since 1988.

Seeing the neon marquee lit up always adds some excitement to attending an evening show here. While the front entrance area still retains the drop ceiling from an earlier renovation, look left for a place where they've taken the ceiling tile out, so you can gaze up at the decorative ceiling hidden above. Someday I hope it is revealed in its entirety!

The Keswick's auditorium has seating for 1300 and is considered to be one of the most "acoustically perfect" venues in the Philadelphia area, making it a destination for touring live acts of all kinds. Looking towards the stage note the two "Sea Goddesses" on the carved screens that obscure the pipes for the theatre organ, hidden on stage right (and only played occasionally.)

From the curved staircase in the lobby you can ogle the colorful mural of maidens, partially obscured by fanciful mid-century modern chandeliers, part of an earlier update to the theater. When on the second level don't forget to appreciate the ornate plasterwork ceiling preserved above the theater offices.

Make night of it and visit The Blue Comet beforehand - you'll feel like you're on a Retro RoadDate for sure!

Keswick Theatre

291 N Keswick Ave
Glenside, PA 19038
(215) 572-7650
www.keswicktheatre.com

15

 ## Mod Betty® Says:

* Peek at the auditorium floor for circular cutouts - those once were vents to cool before air conditioning!

* The Keswick was placed on the National Register of Historic Places in 1983

* Designed by Horace Trumbauer, who also designed the Philadelphia Art Museum

Scan the Stamp!
for map, website and additional info!

PhillyBurbs

Tag your photos from your visit
#RetroRoadmapPHILLYBURBS

Date: / /

My Visit: _____

_____
_____
_____
_____
_____
_____
_____
_____
_____
_____
_____
_____
_____
_____
_____
_____
_____
_____

MONTGOMERY COUNTY

Don't forget to check it off The List!

Lou's Sandwich Shop *Norristown, PA*

Philadelphia may be famous for the hoagie, but for a taste of the little-known regional sandwich known as a Zep, Mod Betty is sending you to Lou's Sandwich Shop in Norristown. Located on busy East Main Street since 1941, you can't miss their iconic logo - a wide mawed gent requesting someone to "Please Pass Me Those Delicious Sandwiches…" - I hope in all these years someone has!

A Zep is made with cooked salami, a thick slice of onion, tomato, oil and oregano, served on a "Conshy roll" (local bread roll from the Conshohocken Bakery.) If you want to put a bit more pep into your zep, hoagie spread made with spicy hot peppers is available at your table.

There are plenty of other sandwiches on the menu - including hoagies and cheesesteaks, but also soups, salads and even milkshakes made on a classic Hamilton Beach mixer.

You have your seating choice of stool at the curved counter, or booth seating at the narrow wooden booths. Heading back towards the booths on the "balcony" you'll spy brothers Lou and Charles Alba busy behind the grill. Their grandfather started the business and they're the last of the family line to keep the tradition going.

Speaking of tradition, you'll quickly realize that a trip to Lou's is a tradition, for locals arriving for their daily fix, or folks who have moved away, returning for a taste of back home. Do yourself a favor and pass them one of those delicious sandwiches, won't you?

Lou's Sandwich Shop

414 E Main St
Norristown, PA 19401
(610) 279-5415
www.facebook.com/Lous-Steak-
Shop-200030190016954

16

Date: / /

My Visit: _____

 Mod Betty® Says:

✳ *Early bird? Breakfast is served 5:30 'til 11am!*

✳ *The gent on the sign is rumored to be inspired by actor Joe E. Brown*

✳ *When in town, check out the interior of the Airy St. Post Office (WPA Mural!)*

Scan the Stamp!
for map, website and additional info!

PhillyBurbs

Tag your photos from your visit
#RetroRoadmapPHILLYBURBS

MONTGOMERY COUNTY

Don't forget to check it off The List!

Ott's Exotic Plants
Schwenksville, PA

As you drive on Route 29 in Schwenksville you'll see a giant glass conservatory building with a domed top stretching 50 feet into the air, and you have to pull over. While you may not find one of the characters from the game of Clue inside, you will find an amazing assortment of plants and flowers, and depending on the season...Mum Mountain.

Ott's Exotic Plants was opened by Godfrey Ott in 1964 with the retail business housed in the stone and slate main building that you see today with its roof sadly swathed in plastic. The business is still owned and operated by the Ott family, who have expanded the indoor greenhouses to include the aforementioned conservatory, which houses an indoor waterfall and two-story tall palm trees!

You'll find boulder-sized ferns hanging from the ceiling of the main greenhouse, but don't worry, there are plenty of regular home sized plants and containers available for purchase as well.

"Mum Mountain" was created from the giant pile of dirt leftover from building the greenhouses and parking lots. In the spring it is covered with flowers just in time for Mother's Day, and in the autumn it is laden with mums. Climb to the top for a beautiful view!

Ott's is not just an attraction, but a place to get all of your gardening needs - and a nice dose of greenery in the wintertime. So if you need fall mums, Christmas poinsettias, Valentines plants, Easter lilies, you "ott" to go to Ott's!

Ott's Exotic Plants (17)

861 Gravel Pike
Schwenksville, PA 19473
(610) 287-7878

 Mod Betty® Says:

✳ *Are you a cat fan? keep your eyes peeled for the greenhouse kitties*

✳ *If you've got a black thumb like Mod B. they also sell decorative planters*

✳ *Wander around here in the winter to absorbe some well needed chlorophyll!*

Scan the Stamp!
for map, website and additional info!

Tag your photos from your visit
#RetroRoadmapPHILLYBURBS

PhillyBurbs

Date: / /

My Visit: _____

_____

_____

_____

_____

_____

_____

_____

_____

_____

_____

_____

_____

_____

_____

_____

_____

MONTGOMERY COUNTY

Don't forget to check it off The List!

Speck's Drive-In Restaurant *Collegeville, PA*

Located smackdab between Pikes (Germantown and Ridge) Speck's Drive-In has been serving up tasty food at this location since 1965. The restaurant is still owned and operated by the family of Stanley "Speck" Landis, who founded the restaurant in 1953.

There are signs on either Pike to guide you into their parking lot - and interestingly, there's no signage on the building itself. White with a red roof, it is reminiscent of a small Howard Johnson's, but with a different paint job. The signs, showing a dapper chicken with a top hat, would make any Retro Roadmap fan detour immediately to investigate.

If the sign didn't clue you in, the menu sure will - Speck's is all about the Broasted chicken. There are other items on the menu like cheeseburgers, hoagies, soups and daily specials. But oh, that chicken! Crispy on the outside, moist on the inside, consider ordering a dinner, for the not-often-seen crinkle cut fries or perhaps the more traditional mashed potatoes as a side.

Do you see what else is cool about Speck's? Just take a look at that Nelson-esque starburst pattern on that table, it's just the start. There was a fire in Specks around 1973 and they remodeled the place then, giving it a colorful orange and yellow palette. This color scheme matches their orange drink, which is a fave thirst quencher for many.

Speck's is Mod Betty's go-to place whenever she doesn't want to cook (and heck I never want to cook, so I'm all set!)

Speck's Drive-In Restaurant 18

3969 Ridge Pike
Collegeville, PA 19426
(610) 489-2110
http://www.speckschicken.com

Date: / /

My Visit: _____

MONTGOMERY COUNTY

Don't forget to check it off The List!

Mod Betty® Says:

❋ *Check out the clock, and those lights, and that paneling, and, and...and!*

❋ *Remind them how much you dig the decor, so they don't think of changing it!*

❋ *They serve chili, but only on Wednesdays*

Scan the Stamp!
for map, website and additional info!

PhillyBurbs

Tag your photos from your visit
#RetroRoadmapPHILLYBURBS

Stutz Candy *Hatboro, PA*

When you're in Hatboro visiting Daddypops, Burdick's or some of the other shops in town, if the sweet tooth strikes, then Stutz Candy is just around the corner. Why sure, you could just pick up a national-brand candy bar any place, but the fun thing about visiting this Stutz Candy shop is that it is located at the factory where they make their own "own make" candy.

You can't miss the giant whitewashed building with bright red signs boldly advertising Rich Creamy Fudge, Buttery Peanut Brittle and The Largest and Finest Variety of Candies, so pull into the parking lot and head into the retail section.

There you will find chocolates, candies and nuts literally lining the walls. Boxes with colorful bows are ready for gift giving, or you can assemble your own assortment by making a selection from the glass cases. Note that not every single piece of candy for sale is actually made here, so if you're curious, just ask.

In operation since 1938, this "Own Make" candy company was started by Joe and Mary Stutz, and in the 1960s purchased by Dairy Maid Confectionery. John Glaser, a 3rd generation candy maker from Dairy Maid took over the operation, moving the candy making to this location in 1976. Today his nephew (5th generation!) continues the tradition.

There are two additional locations of Stutz, one in Warminster and on the Jersey Shore on Long Beach Island. But for an unexpected shopping experience off the beaten path, this is a sweet spot.

Stutz Candy　⑲

400 S Warminster Rd
Hatboro, PA 19040
(215) 675-2632
www.stutzcandy.com

 Mod Betty® Says:

❋ *Don't you just love the old fashioned "Own Make" terminology? I do!*

❋ *Check out their wall of molded chocolates! Spell your name or buy a chocolate cellphone*

❋ *Don't forget to tune into WRDV-FM 89.3 to listen to big band, jazz and swing - they're located in downtown Hatboro!*

Scan the Stamp!
for map, website and additional info!

PhillyBurbs

Tag your photos from your visit
#RetroRoadmapPHILLYBURBS

Date: ___/___/___

My Visit: _____

_____

_____

_____

_____

_____

_____

_____

_____

_____

_____

_____

_____

_____

_____

_____

MONTGOMERY COUNTY

Don't forget to check it off The List!

Waltz Golf Farm

Limerick, PA

Mod Betty's not the athletic type, so the vintage miniature golf course at Waltz Golf Farm is her version of a workout. A swell retro destination for the entire family, it offers 2 miniature golf courses, 9 hole par 3 golf, driving range, batting cages, and even gemstone panning. But the main draw here for Retro Roadmap is the original Farm course.

In 1964 the Waltz family converted their corn farm into this golf center, and the Farm course has many of the classic things you'd expect from old timey miniature golf of that era. There's a bridge, a wishing well, a school house with doors that open and close, and more. Note, there's no windmill, but the wheelbarrow tips!

Though some folks may prefer the more modern Castle mini golf with its waterfalls and castle, I'm happy to see that Waltz's still has kept and maintained the old fashioned obstacles with quaint touches like the stone Pennsylvania farm house, and the hex sign on the barn. The fact that it is well tended with flowers, trees and a little vegetable "farm" just adds to the charm.

Alas, the snack bar, built in 1972 no longer carries the Broasted chicken that the roadside Pepsi sign touts (but we still love that sign!) In addition to hotdogs and hamburgers they serve Nelson's ice cream (Mod B's fave local ice cream), made right down the street in Royersford so you can celebrate your mini-golf victories with a sweet treat!

Waltz Golf Farm

20

303 W Ridge Pike
Limerick, PA 19468
(610) 489-7859
www.waltzgolffarm.com

Date: / /

My Visit: _____

Mod Betty® Says:

✺ *Waltz hosts an annual 4th of July bash for the community - fireworks and everything!*

✺ *Listen for the kids singing when the school door opens and closes*

✺ *They've got party packages for kids, and special rates for seniors*

MONTGOMERY COUNTY

Don't forget to check it off The List!

Scan the Stamp!
for map, website and additional info!

PhillyBurbs

Tag your photos from your visit
#RetroRoadmapPHILLYBURBS

Weitzenkorn's Men's Store *Pottstown, PA*

Though you, like Mod Betty, may not need a men's suit at the moment, Weitzenkorn's Men's Store is worth a visit. Not only is it the second-oldest* family run mens store in the country, but oh, that neon sign! Its yellow neon script brightens up downtown Pottstown and is a landmark, day or night.

The business began in 1864 and is now run by 4th and 5th generation Weitzenkorn men. This history can be seen throughout the shop, especially in the glass case displaying ads and store ephemera from decades gone by.

If you are in the market for a new suit or dress shirt, Weitzenkorn's will be able to outfit you, no matter what your size. Custom shirts can be made from a variety of fabrics, and there's a tailor on staff to ensure you're well fitted. Need a tuxedo for a wedding? You can rent them here as well.

Not all of the clothing is formal here at Weitzenkorns, so if you are looking for something more casual, use this as an excuse to visit the lower level. Here you'll not only find Tommy Bahama clothing, but also be able to view the tubes from the antique pneumatic cashier system.

The historic plaque outside of the shop notes that in 1889 the first private electric lamp in Pottstown was installed in Weitzenkorn's. While Mod Betty knows it's not the case, she'd like to imagine that lamp was the Alligator All Weather Coats lamp on display in the front of the store.

Weitzenkorn's Men's Store

21

145 E High St
Pottstown, PA 19464
(610) 323-8810
www.weitzenkorns.com

Date: / /

My Visit: _____

MONTGOMERY COUNTY

Don't forget to check it off The List!

Mod Betty® Says:

* *The oldest men's store is Levy's in Nashville, started in 1855*

* *Don't forget to check out the painted sign on the side of the brick building*

* *If they're not too busy, ask them to pull out the chrome racks from the wall - ingenious!*

Scan the Stamp!
for map, website and additional info!

PhillyBurbs

Tag your photos from your visit
#RetroRoadmapPHILLYBURBS

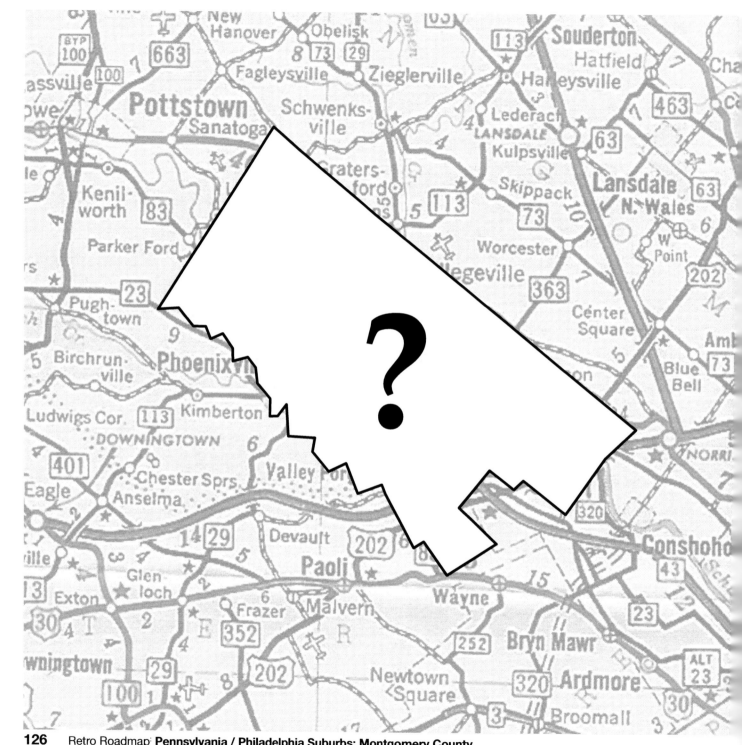

_____

_____

_____

_____

_____

_____

_____

_____

_____

_____

_____

_____

_____

_____

_____

_____

_____

_____

_____

_____

_____

_____

Index
Pennsylvania-Philadelphia Suburbs

BY BUSINESS NAME/TOWN

Index

Pennsylvania-Philadelphia Suburbs

BY TOWN/BUSINESS NAME